Pot
Shots
at
Poetry

Poets on Poetry   Donald Hall, General Editor

DONALD HALL	*Goatfoot Milktongue Twinbird*
GALWAY KINNELL	*Walking Down the Stairs*
WILLIAM STAFFORD	*Writing the Australian Crawl*
DONALD DAVIE	*Trying to Explain*
MAXINE KUMIN	*To Make a Prairie*
DIANE WAKOSKI	*Toward a New Poetry*
ROBERT BLY	*Talking All Morning*
ROBERT FRANCIS	*Pot Shots at Poetry*
DAVID IGNATOW	*Open Between Us*
RICHARD KOSTELANETZ	*The Old Poetries and the New*
LOUIS SIMPSON	*A Company of Poets*
PHILIP LEVINE	*Don't Ask*
JOHN HAINES	*Living Off the Country*
MARGE PIERCY	*Parti-Colored Blocks for a Quilt*
DONALD HALL	*The Weather for Poetry*
JAMES WRIGHT	*Collected Prose*
MARVIN BELL	*Old Snow Just Melting*
ALICIA OSTRIKER	*Writing Like a Woman*
JOHN LOGAN	*A Ballet for the Ear*
HAYDEN CARRUTH	*Effluences from the Sacred Caves*
ROBERT HAYDEN	*Collected Prose*
DONALD JUSTICE	*Platonic Scripts*
JOHN FREDERICK NIMS	*A Local Habitation*
ANNE SEXTON	*No Evil Star*
CHARLES SIMIC	*The Uncertain Certainty*

Pot Shots at Poetry

ROBERT FRANCIS

Ann Arbor   The University of Michigan Press

1989   1988   1987   1986   5   4   3   2

Library of Congress Cataloging in Publication Data

Francis, Robert, 1901-
    Pot shots at poetry.

    (Poets on poetry)
    I. Title.   II. Series.
PS3511.R237P6   809.1   79-23988
ISBN 0-472-06318-9

Grateful acknowledgment is made to the following publishers:

The University of Massachusetts Press for permission to re-
print *The Satirical Rogue on Poetry*, originally published by The
University of Massachusetts Press in 1968 under the same title.
Copyright © 1968 by Robert Francis.

Tunnel Press for an interview with Robert Francis conducted
by Philip Tetreault and Kathy Sewalk-Karcher originally published by Tunnel Press in 1976 as *Francis on the Spot*. Copyright © 1976 by Robert Francis. Poems included in this interview copyright © 1936, 1964, 1965, 1970, 1972, 1974 by
Robert Francis.

To my dear wife, Patience

"I see myself walking round and round Poetry on its pedestal and taking shots at it from every possible angle. Shots with a light gun, a water pistol, or a pea shooter."

Contents

I. THE SATIRICAL ROGUE ON POETRY

Be Brutal   *3*
Either Or   *4*
On Looking Like a Poet   *5*
Blood   *6*
Defense of Poetry   *7*
Lyric as Arrow   *8*
Black Eye   *9*
In Her Own Right   *10*
On the Exquisite Air   *11*
Distinction   *12*
Teacher   *13*
The Muse   *14*
Poetic License   *15*
Scenes   *17*
Poet as Bird   *18*
Art of Slow Reading   *19*
Word-Count   *20*
Half-God   *22*
Garret   *23*
Love Me, Love My Poems   *24*
It Really Isn't   *25*
Bad Poem   *26*
With and without Honorarium   *28*
Lounge   *29*
Frost as Mugwump   *30*
Poetry as a Source of Suffering   *32*
By the Rude Bridge That Arched the Flood   *34*
Production Belt   *36*
Labels   *38*
Somebody—Nobody   *39*
Santayana, Columbus, and Samuel Eliot Morison   *40*
The Pathetic Fallacy   *41*
The Man Who Wrote One Poem   *44*

†   Dame Edith   *45*

Duty   *46*

Poetry as an Un-American Activity   *48*

Too Busy for Both   *49*

The Messy Muse   *50*

Mr. Eliot's Cats   *51*

Noncriticism   *52*

Wild but Polished   *53*

Goddess   *55*

Advantages in Being a Poet   *56*

No Poem So Fine   *58*

Woman with the Tape Recorder   *59*

Emily and I   *60*

Silent Poetry   *61*

Hard   *63*

Poetry as Stuff   *65*

Lowell   *66*

Poet on the Platform   *67*

Redress of Grievance   *69*

To Dislike Poetry Is Not Necessarily to Disparage It   *70*

Chaos   *71*

First Person Singular   *72*

Poet as Noble Achievement   *74*

Vacations   *75*

The Disillusioning Blurb   *76*

A Golden Simplicity?   *77*

Required Reading   *78*

Professional Poet   *79*

Poetry and Poverty   *80*

The Indecipherable Poem   *82*

Electronically Equipped   *84*

The Satirical Rogue   *85*

Patience and a Monument   *86*

Poetry and Power   *88*

Logic   *89*

John Quincy Adams   *90*

Publisher as Wife   *92*

Style   *93*

Poetry as a Competitive Pursuit   *94*
The Well-made Poem   *95*
Crowds   *96*
Modest Check   *97*
Group Reviews   *98*
Yarrow   *99*
Weighed in the Balance   *100*
A Small Door   *101*
Other Arts, Other Artists   *102*
Peacock   *105*
In a Brazen World   *106*
Slender   *107*
Introducing the Poet   *108*

II.   WHAT A WITCH TOLD ME

III.   FRANCIS ON THE SPOT
An Interview: With Philip Tetreault and
    Kathy Sewalk-Karcher   *121*

IV.   THE SATIRICAL ROGUE AGAIN
Two Words   *149*
Confetti Poet   *150*
Sedentary   *151*
Critic   *152*
Major   *154*
Poetry as Work   *155*
Energy   *156*
Poems as Apples   *157*
My Life   *158*
Caught in a Corner   *159*
The Trouble with Pegasus   *160*
Poetry   *161*
Neither   *162*
Anthologists   *163*
The Disposable Poem   *165*
Wordman   *166*
The Multipurpose Room   *167*

Poet as Parrot   *168*
Lemuel Beaver   *169*
Poetry Workshop   *170*
A Little Thinking   *171*
The Puritan in Me   *172*
A Passable Sonnet   *173*
Computers   *174*
Towers   *175*
The Death of Poetry   *176*
J. P. K.   *178*
Will No One Stand Up for the Adjective?   *179*
An Experiment   *180*
Dates   *183*
Handwriting   *184*
Deception   *185*
The Great World   *186*
The Robert Poets   *187*
Francis   *188*
Hardihood   *189*
Collected Poems   *190*
A Lucky Generation   *191*
The *New Yorker* Home Treasury of Verse   *192*
To Wield the Pen   *193*
Golden Edith   *194*
The Reversible Dictum   *195*
A Wide Wide World   *196*
Horticulture   *197*
On the Moon   *198*
Gift Copies   *200*
Theophilus Again   *201*
John Peale Bishop, John Crowe Ransom, and
    Robert Penn Warren   *202*
Invoice to Go with a Gift Copy of My Poems   *203*
E. D.   *204*
Magic   *205*
Emily   *206*
Again the Rose   *207*
For Queens   *208*

Byron, Kelly, and Sheets   *209*
Landor   *210*
The Discoverer   *211*
Yes, Why?   *212*
Festivals   *213*
Elegy   *214*
Luxury Cruise   *215*
A League   *216*
Friends of the Francis   *217*
Local Poet   *218*

I

The Satirical Rogue on Poetry

Polonius: I'll speak to him again. What do you read, my lord?

Hamlet: Words, words, words.

Polonius: What is the matter, my lord?

Hamlet: Between who?

Polonius: I mean, the matter that you read, my lord.

Hamlet: Slanders, sir: for the satirical rogue says here that old men have gray beards, etc.

[*Hamlet, 2.2*]

Be Brutal

A friend comes with poems to be criticized. "Be brutal," he says. "Be ruthless. Tear them apart."

You smile and take the poems in your hand. Be brutal? Somehow you never feel brutal toward a poem, even when it obviously deserves brutality. Toward a human being, perhaps, now and then, but not toward a poem. It lies there on the page so helpless to defend itself, so at your mercy. After all, it is only a few inoffensive words put together in a certain way.

No, you could never be really brutal with a poem. And you suspect that he knows you couldn't. What he really wants and hopes is that you will love his poems and praise them. But he wants to keep as far as possible from seeming to. He wants your praise to surprise him. He wants to say he didn't think the poems were very good himself. Ideally he himself would like to be brutal while you triumphantly defended his poems. "Be brutal," he says.

Pulling yourself together, you resolve to be helpful, tactful, and honest, all at the same time. You recall the critics of *your* poetry who were only honest. Particularly one man who lit his pipe and took a puff and said, "The trouble with this poem—" And took another puff and said, "The trouble with this poem—" And took another puff and said, "The trouble with this poem—"

So you ask your friend if he would be willing to leave the poems with you for a day or two. You want to brood over them.

"Okay," he says. "But be brutal."

Either Or

"After talking with Uncle Charles the other night about the worthies of this country, Webster and the rest, as usual, considering who were geniuses and who not, I showed him up to bed," says Thoreau in his *Journal* for January 1, 1853, "and when I had got into bed myself, I heard his chamber door opened after eleven o'clock, and he called out, in an earnest, stentorian voice, loud enough to wake the whole house, 'Henry! was John Quincy Adams a genius?' 'No I think not,' was my reply. 'Well, I didn't think he was,' answered he."

Whether Henry and Uncle Charles agreed on any other worthies, there was something they seem to have agreed on implicitly and that was that a man is either a genius or not a genius.

Isn't this a little odd in a man who measured accurately the varying depth of Walden Pond and the varying thickness of Walden ice? Did it never enter his immensely capable head that genius, though it cannot be measured like ice and water, is nevertheless something that varies in amount, like water and ice, from spot to spot and individual to individual? That while most people have none to speak of and a few have it in abundance, some people have genius in small amounts? Did it never occur to him that John Quincy Adams was a great man with possibly a small amount of genius? Less than Daniel Webster but more than John Doe down the road?

Another night Henry and Uncle Charles may have discussed the poets, who were major and who minor, putting all the poets into their respective hemispheres separated by a line as inexorable and as imaginary as the equator.

On Looking Like a Poet

Some poets look like poets, other poets do not, but those who do do not all look the same. There was the big blue beret and the small red beard. There was also the great white head and the black overcoat slung over the shoulders like a cloak. Sometimes a poet looks like a poet without trying.

Interesting to speculate why some poets do and some poets do not, why some want to and others don't care or even want not to. If looking like a poet can be an advantage, it can also be a disadvantage. The difference depends on what sort of poet the poet is looking like, and also on where he happens to be. For some poets it would take courage to look like a poet, but the courage might prove unrewarding.

Self-expression is important to all poets, and looking like a poet is one form of it. If a poet happens not to be writing fine poems or even any poems at all, looking like a poet may be almost the only form of self-expression he has.

Blood

"You have a stain on your white shirt," said my friend. "Looks like blood which the laundry couldn't take out."

"It's blood all right," I said. "I got it at a recent poetry reading."

"My God!" he cried, "are poets now wielding knives and rapiers?"

"Not the poets but their poems," I answered. "This fellow's were so violent and bloody there was danger of getting spattered if you sat too near the front."

"I suppose you didn't object to the blood and violence," he went on, "but only to the getting spattered."

"Maybe," I murmured.

Defense of Poetry

I knew a poet once who defended poetry. He defended poetry as he would have defended womanhood on the highway at night. Actually he did more than defend poetry, he defended individual poems. Thus he went beyond Shelley and Sidney who were content to defend poetry in general and in the abstract. One might almost say there never was a poem this poet wouldn't defend. None was too poor or frail for him to champion. Frailty rather than beauty it must have often been that roused his chivalry.

If a slip of a high-school girl wrote an "Ode to Spring," this poet instantly became protective. Any poem, any poem at all, by the fact of its being a poem was precious and therefore precarious.

He was a rare bird. Possibly no one today feels and acts just as he did.

Certainly not I. I would say that a poem worth defending needs no defense and a poem needing defense is not worth defending. I would say it is not our business to defend poetry but the business of poetry to defend us.

Lyric as Arrow

It goes without saying that an arrow to wound must be well aimed; to wound cleanly must be sharply pointed; and to fly accurately through the air must be light, slender, and tough. May not much the same be said of a lyric?

Of any brief poem that we today call a lyric? And doesn't the scarcity of these arrowlike qualities help to explain why I am so often bruised by a poem, so seldom wounded cleanly?

And I want to be wounded. Like Sebastian I bare my breast to the arrows. I would gather them in. I am already sufficiently bruised.

Black Eye

A drawing of Pablo Neruda by Seymour Leichman (repro-
duced in the *New York Times Book Review* of July 10,
1966) shows the Chilean poet with a pronounced black
eye. But it was only recently that the significance of this
feature came home to me.

What is a poet, after all, but someone to whom life has
given a black eye? How better could you define him?

One poet will simply report the fact, as vividly as he
can. A second poet will go beyond reporting to express an
acceptance or a reconciliation in the sense that Margaret
Fuller accepted the universe. A third poet is the rebel
boasting that if life has given him a black eye he has
done the same to life.

Poets, of course, also write poems. But without the
black eye no writer of poems is ever quite the poet.

In Her Own Right

Whenever I hear of someone who is a poet in her own right or in his own right, I am curious to know in what other way a person can ever be a poet.

Take Cornelia Crumb, for instance, wife of the poet Crumb, who we are informed is a poet in her own right.

The implication is that Mrs. Crumb is a poet in her own right in addition to being a poet in a right not her own. But if being the wife of a poet confers quasipoethood on Mrs. Crumb, why isn't this in her own right too, since Crumb is without question her husband?

If I were writing about Mrs. Crumb I would say: "Mrs. Crumb is a poet too." Or, "Mrs. Crumb, like her husband, is a poet." Or, "Mrs. Crumb is a poet herself."

But no one else thinks as I do. Let anybody else write about Mrs. Crumb and we are assured that she is a poet in her own right.

On the Exquisite Air

All artists love to talk about themselves and their art, but poets in their public readings seem unable or unwilling even for a few minutes to separate their art from themselves.

They give us details of inspiration, composition, and publication. They go behind the scenes and take us with them. What we have is nothing less than a complete poet's-eye view of his poems.

Sometimes the commentary and confession come in such an engulfing stream that the poems are quite submerged and only dart in and out of sight like swimming fish.

Why poets do so much talking in public I really don't know. In his studio a painter may or may not chat about his paintings; but when those paintings are hung in an exhibit, does he post himself at the door to give every visitor a personally conducted tour?

My own notion of a poetry reading is quite different. I want the poet to talk about his poems as little as possible, and not so much about the poems as about something one step removed. The voice in which he does his talking unfortunately is the same voice the poor poems must borrow. The more we hear him the less we may be able to hear them.

I should like poems hung, one at a time, like Japanese pictures, on the exquisite air, each poem surrounded by space and silence.

Distinction

Finding themselves at last together in one book, the poems accepted each other almost instantly. After all, were they not a true family, having one and the same father?

Those that had had the honor of previous publication in magazines and those that were appearing in print for the first time soon forgot their differences of status.

All except one little poem—and you couldn't tell merely by looking at it why it was this little poem and not any other little poem in the book. But it was a fact that this little poem had first appeared in the *New Yorker* and it could never quite forget it.

Teacher

When I look back at the poetry teaching I have done or tried to do, I see it in the form of a round pie cut in six sections.

The first slice is what I told them that they already knew. This generally pleased them since it made them feel like advanced students.

The second slice is what I told them that they could have found out just as well or better from books. What, for instance, is a sestina?

The third slice is what I told them that they refused to accept. I could see it on their faces, and later I saw the evidence in their writing.

The fourth slice is what I told them that they were willing to accept and may have thought they accepted but couldn't accept since they couldn't fully understand. This also I saw in their faces and in their work. Here, no doubt, I was mostly to blame.

The fifth slice is what I told them that they discounted as whimsey or something simply to fill up time. After all, I was being paid to talk.

The sixth slice is what I didn't tell them, for I didn't try to tell them all I knew. Deliberately I kept back something—a few professional secrets, a magic formula or two.

So my pie is all used up and what teaching have I done?

Yet we always had a good time in class. Drawn together by a common interest and pursuit, we enjoyed one another's company. Especially we enjoyed laughing together.

The Muse

When people speak of The Bard everyone knows they mean Shakespeare. But when people speak of The Muse which Muse do they mean? For there are no fewer than nine Muses, as who hasn't heard? Nine daughters of Zeus and Mnemosyne, the goddess of Memory.

Calliope, *epic poetry*
Clio, *history*
Erato, *erotic poetry*
Euterpe, *lyric poetry*
Melpomene, *tragedy*
Polyhymnia, *religious poetry*
Terpsichore, *the dance*
Thalia, *comedy or bucolic poetry*
Urania, *astronomy*

After eliminating Clio, Terpsichore, and Urania, we still have six. Why do people persist in talking as if there were only one Muse when there are six of these divine women ready, each in her proper field and jurisdiction, to come to the aid of the deserving poet?

Poetic License

How many years has it been since I heard that phrase? And just what does it mean, or did it mean? Does it, did it, refer to a general latitude permitted poets in their use of language, or did it refer to something more specific? I think I used to know. But that was long ago.

What did my high school English teacher have to say about poetic license? Was it poetic license when a poet said "marge" for "margin"? Or was it something else? I'm sure she knew and made us know; but though I remember some things she taught us as if it were yesterday, I have forgotten what she said about poetic license.

I remember very well the Harvard Comma, for instance. When three or more words are used in a series, the first two are separated from each other by a comma. The last two are separated (as well as connected) by the word "and." Should there be a comma here too? For years the question had hung fire, some authorities saying one thing, other authorities another. But now Harvard had spoken. There *should* be a comma before the "and." Red, white, and blue. This was the Harvard Comma.

Hila Helen Small was an extraordinarily devoted and conscientious teacher. It would be no exaggeration to say no human being could have been more so. I remember her as entirely gray—not only hair and eyes but manner and speech. She moved swiftly through the corridors with a soft swish and a faint jingling of keys.

Actually she was not quite so severe as she looked. Her severity was not so much toward human beings as toward what they said and wrote. Once, for instance, she appeared suddenly in a room that had been left temporarily teacherless. There she stood in perfect silence, her gray eyes fixed on a small misbehaving girl. "The boy in back of me hit me with his ruler," said the child in defense.

What would Avenging Justice say to this? What punishment would be meted out?

"Never say 'in back of,' say 'behind,' " said Miss Small.

Early in life she had taken a vow that no ungrammatical or otherwise incorrect expression should ever pass her lips and none ever had. We, her pupils, could watch the unending struggle, the pursed lips, the poised teeth. Miss Small never said anything bright, or profound, or amusing, but, by God, she never said anything incorrect.

Today when the attitude toward language is almost altogether permissive, we smile at such perfectionism. But we may be missing something, just the same. There was excitement in Miss Small's correctness. It was like a game. Would she or wouldn't she ever make a slip?

But what did she tell us about poetic license? I'm sure it was the most unlicentious kind of license imaginable. I still use the Harvard Comma regularly, though during my five years at Harvard I never once heard it mentioned.

Scenes

I

A: Did I see a poem of yours somewhere recently?
I: It's possible.
A: Where could it have been?
I: What magazine was it in?
A: I don't remember.
I: About how long ago was it?
A: I've forgotten.
I: Do you recall the title?
A: No.
I: Or what the poem was about?
A: No.
I: Or anything about the poem?
A: Oh, it doesn't make that much difference. I just wanted you to know I'd seen it.

II

B: Did I see a poem of yours somewhere recently?
I: Impossible.
B: I'm sure it had your name.
I: Must have been the other Robert Francis who writes poetry.

Poet as Bird

"This," says The Yale Series of Recorded Poets of Yvor Winters, "is a field recording made in the poet's own locale."

Art of Slow Reading

The more we race over the surface of the earth and the faster and farther we fly above it the more important now and then to do a little walking.

In an age of speed reading, poetry has the virtue, in addition to whatever other virtues, of slowing us down. A shrewd doctor might prescribe the reading of poetry for a variety of contemporary ills.

Poetry, of course, has always been something to read slowly, just as a fine wine has always been something to sip. But today, as everyone knows, there is another reason for slow going. In the past you grasped a poem fairly quickly and lingered over it for enjoyment. Today you often have to linger over a poem to grasp it at all.

By slow reading we generally mean not only a slow pace but a frequent pausing and a going back to read again. Rapid reading is measured by so many words a minute or second. It would be absurd to try to measure slow reading. Yet one might say sensibly that in a flight to Chicago he spent the two hours reading one short poem.

I hope it was not a mere puzzle-poem. A puzzle-poem might keep one reading all the way to the moon and back. Ideally one would spend most of the two hours not so much trying to penetrate the poem's shell as its depth. One would muse over not only what the poem was saying but what the poem was doing.

Slow reading of this sort is a double test: a test of the reader's resources and a test of the poem's. Poem asks the reader: "Do you get all I am giving?" Reader asks the poem: "How long can you keep me interested, keep me reading? All the way to Chicago?"

Word-Count

Daphnis: Seen any of the so-called word-count poems that Robert Francis writes?

Damon: Not that I know of. What's the idea?

Daphnis: All the lines in a poem have the same number of words. It might be seven to a line, or five, or perhaps only three.

Damon: I couldn't get excited about that.

Daphnis: It doesn't have to be exciting to be useful. Question is, can it help produce a fine poem?

Damon: Daphnis my boy, fine poems are sometimes, by the grace of God, produced in spite of rather than because of artificial frameworks.

Daphnis: That's a debatable point, Damon. I mean, what you call *in spite of* may actually be *because of*. A poem gets written in spite of something or other. Because of in spite of, you might say.

Damon: God, what quibbling! But it's not quibbling to say that counting words is too mechanical.

Daphnis: Any more mechanical than counting feet? Five feet to the line? Five words to a line?

Damon: But feet are meter and meter means rhythm and rhythm is the lifeblood of poetry. Counting words is like counting sausages.

Daphnis: All right, I grant you that counting words does nothing for the rhythm. But how about counting syllables? As Marianne Moore does? Don't some pretty brilliant poems get written that way? Because of or in spite of?

Damon: Oh, if you have to count something, syllables will do. They're short.

Daphnis: But why not words? Playing the long ones against the short ones?

Damon: That's precisely what all poets do anyhow.

Daphnis: Damon, old boy, we're arguing. But the proof of a poem is in the reading.

Damon: Have you got one on you?

Daphnis: Yes. I copied it at the library this morning. *[Takes out a folded paper and hands it to Damon.]* It's typical Francis.

Icicles

Only a fierce
Coupling begets them
Fire and freezing

Only from violent
Yet gentle parents
Their baroque beauty

Under the sun
Their life passes
But wait awhile

Under the moon
They are finished
Works of art

Poems in print
Yet pity them
Only by wasting

Away they grow
And their death
Is pure violence.

Damon: Sort of brittle, I'd say. But then you'd have to remark that so are icicles.

Daphnis: Damon, old scout, you're hard to please.

Damon: And you, Daphnis, I sometimes think are too easy.

Half-God

How Socrates must have surprised that drinking party over two thousand years ago when he told them that the god of love was not a god who had everything, but rather a half-god always longing to complete himself.

Isn't a poet typically the same? If his wife can't think of anything to give him for Christmas, it isn't because he already has everything, but only because what he doesn't have his wife can't give him.

Or perhaps he has no wife. If he is so poor that he goes hungry, he will probably somehow or other be rich in love. Or if he is starved for love, he will doubtless sit down to a good dinner every day.

If he had everything, what impulse would he have to write? If he had nothing, what would he write about?

Garret

It has just occurred to me, after all these years, that my basic lack as a poet may have come from my not having a garret to live in and write in, to sleep in and dream in.

Where better than in a garret can a poet be both high and humble? An integral part of life and yet above it all? From a garret he can look out on treetops and across to other garrets. He can look down on the bustling world and yet not too far down. In spring and summer and fall he can listen to the rain's commentary close to his head, and in winter he can watch the lengthening icicles as they dazzle in sun or glint in moon.

If some philanthropic foundation, or indeed if my country itself, wishes to grant me some signal boon, rather than gold or travelers checks let them give me a garret to live in and write in, to sleep in and dream in.

But what am I saying? This is not the way to get a garret. To get a garret—if haply there are any garrets left in the modern world—one should find it himself and pay the rent with money he himself earns. That would be good in every way you look at it.

Love Me, Love My Poems

Long, long ago this was my good fortune. When my first book was published, everyone who knew me knew that book. Everyone who was betting on me bet on me as a poet. Everyone who loved me loved my handiwork. Not that I made demands on my friends. Their pleasure in my flowering was as spontaneous as if the flowering were their own.

How different it is now. How very, very different now.

It Really Isn't

It isn't expensive to be a poet. A pencil and piece of paper are all the equipment needed to get started. Homer managed with less.

A pencil or pen and a few pieces of paper. Then an envelope or two and some postage stamps.

Pencil or pen or typewriter. A portable typewriter isn't expensive if you can make one last a lifetime.

You may fancy writing in an Italian villa or a French château, but the poems you write there will be no more immortal than those written in your bedroom at home.

Nor do you need very much of that most precious of all items, time. Odds and ends will do. Evenings, early mornings, noon hours. Sundays, holidays, and when you sprain your ankle.

It's quite otherwise with a painter. Paints, brushes, and canvases cost money, and a painter can't very well paint in his bedroom. Still less could a sculptor sculpt in a bedroom. An architect may need a whole suite of rooms in an office building. And as for the composer, what can he do without a grand piano and somewhere to play it?

No, if a poet can support himself he can support his poetry. If he can keep himself fed, his poems won't starve.

So, when you come right down to brass tacks, a poet doesn't really need the aid, assistance, subsidy, and support that munificent philanthropy stands ready to grant him. In this, isn't he lucky?

If you insist on giving him something, say, a free year in Rome, it may turn out that what you have chiefly done is to add to his baggage.

Bad Poem

There are two approved ways of turning thumbs down on a poem. (1) You can say it isn't a poem at all. It's merely verse. It's doggerel. It's mere rhetoric. Or (2) you can call it a bad poem.

Either way disposes of a poem effectively, but only in the second way can you properly send it to hell. A poem that isn't a poem at all, a poem that is merely verse or doggerel or rhetoric, does not necessarily deserve eternal torment. After all, verse has its place. Even doggerel has its place. Rhetoric may not have any place today but it used to have and so enjoys an honorable background. But a bad poem obviously deserves to be cast into outer darkness where there is weeping and gnashing of teeth.

When you call a poem bad, you pick it up firmly by the ear between thumb and forefinger and toss it into the pit. As you do so you give a shrug, a wry smile, a grimace, as if the poem were not only bad but smelled bad.

If somebody comes along and tries to tell you that there are many, many poems too good to be called bad and too bad to be called good, and that within bad and good there are infinite degrees of badness and goodness, and that a poem may be rather good in some respects and rather bad in others, and that goodness and badness depend on criteria about which poets and critics will never agree, and that a poem might better be called poor, or feeble, or faulty, or unfulfilled than bad—if anybody tries to talk that way, you can be sure he is quibbling, hedging, evading, unwilling honestly to face the responsibilities of judgment.

It is all quite clear and definite. Bad poems are bad,

and poems not bad are good. And just as there are bad poems and good poems, so there are bad poets and good poets. A bad poet probably never writes a good poem, but some admittedly good poets have confessed to writing some bad poems. For a good poet to confess writing a bad poem tends to prove three things: (1) his candor, (2) his critical acumen, and (3) the goodness of all his good poems.

But why split hairs? Have not the estimable authors of *Understanding Poetry* put the whole matter in a nutshell? "Bad poems," they say on page 391, "are made by bad poets like Kilmer and good poems are made by good poets like Yeats, Shakespeare, Milton, etc."

With and without Honorarium

A poet is like a physician in at least one respect. Sometimes he is paid for his services and sometimes not. He may be well paid one night and not at all the next. A physician of course is glad to do work free, or at least he takes his charity cases in stride. The same thing may well be true of a poet.

When he is working for pay, receiving perhaps several hundred dollars for a reading or lecture, people can't do enough for him. He is met at the airport and taken to someone's home for entertainment overnight. He is guest of honor at a dinner before his reading and at a party afterward. If he has been permitted to incur any expense at all, he will probably be reimbursed for it in addition to his honorarium. Finally, after a leisurely breakfast the next morning, he is taken back to the airport. Again and again he is thanked for coming.

What happens when he is working free? It is probably a local occasion and he is allowed to get there by his own devices. At the door he is met by someone who tells him where he can leave his hat and coat. The audience proves just a trifle cool. The poems that last night seemed to give pleasure give less pleasure now. After it is all over, someone thanks him. He goes out and gets into his car and starts home. On his way he begins to wonder whether he should not have thanked the audience for their kindness in coming.

Lounge

God forbid I ever have to give a poetry reading in a lounge, a lounge where the listener sinks out of sight and sound in some deep-bosomed overstuffed divan.

If anybody ever drops a pin during my reading, for God's sake let me be where I can hear it!

Frost as Mugwump

Years ago I heard Robert Frost define a mugwump as a little bird balancing on a twig with his mug pointing one way and his wump the other. Wasn't Frost himself a perfect illustration?

He laughed at educators, and was one. He twitted scientists but kept up with what they were doing. He was proart and antiart: an artist to his fingertips when writing poems, but a plain man and no nonsense on the platform speaking those poems. Also a plain man and no nonsense speaking *in* those poems. As for religion, you can make out as good a case for Frost the skeptic as for Frost the believer.

He was in favor of walls and he was scornful of walls. In "Mending Wall" the speaker kids his neighbor for insisting on repairing an unnecessary wall; but the speaker keeps right on doing his share of repairing nevertheless. That was not the only fence that Frost was on both sides of.

Did his mugwumpism help him as a poet? I wouldn't venture to say. Some great poets have been middle-of-the-road, others have been extremists. But one thing certain is that his mugwumpism helped Frost as a wise man. In the popular mind a wise man can't be an extremist. If he is so broadly and centrally located that he speaks, or seems to speak, for everybody, then he is a wise man indeed.

Of course Frost's definition of mugwump is far from accurate, and Frost probably only picked it up somewhere. Strictly speaking, a mugwump is a member of one political party who now and then switches his vote to the other party. This is what many Republicans did in 1884 to help elect Grover Cleveland. A mugwump by rights is a little bird that flits back and forth between two twigs. Or that changes his direction on the same twig.

Frost had good reason to be interested in mugwumps, for in politics he was close to being one in the true meaning of the word. A passionate Democrat at nine years of age, he helped elect Cleveland. At eighty-six he not only helped elect another Democrat for President, he helped inaugurate him. But in between, during those New Deal years, that was another story.

My guess is that Frost would not object to being called a mugwump. The word was pure American even before the coming of the white man. In the Algonquin tongue it means "big chief." No, Frost would not object. I can almost hear him chuckle.

Poetry as a Source of Suffering

Only in the secrecy of my own heart do I dare confess how much suffering poetry has brought me over the years. To confess to anyone else would open me to the charge of ingratitude both to the Muse and to my fellow poets. I am really a little ashamed to confess even to myself that what supposedly should have been a source of pleasure has so often been otherwise.

My suffering is of three sorts. My own poetry has made me suffer, and for this, of course, I myself am exclusively to blame. Then I have suffered from what other people have said or not said about my poetry. Finally, there is the suffering from other people's poetry. For this, surely, I am not wholly responsible.

When I speak of the suffering that my own poetry has brought me, I am not thinking of the struggle of creation, for this is a happy kind of agony if it results in something worth agonizing over. I am thinking rather of those poems that brought a glow of achievement one night but disintegrated under my eyes the next morning. Or of those poems that ought to have disintegrated but somehow found their way into print.

What I suffer from in other people's poetry is many things, according to poet and poem. But perhaps most of all from the too obtrusive presence of the poet himself. I want him near enough to see and hear vividly, but not necessarily so near as to feel his breath in my face.

One could argue that it is a chief virtue of poetry today to cause the reader to suffer. To make him accept his suffering and even to enjoy it. Only by prodding him, shocking him, and making him wince can a poet waken and revitalize his reader. I suffer; therefore I am.

If this is so, then I can only say that I wish I could have enjoyed my suffering more.

By the Rude Bridge That Arched the Flood

That such a little jewel of a poem as Emerson's "Concord Hymn" should be an occasional poem is something of a paradox. Though occasional poems occasionally pass muster, they are very very seldom jewels.

Part of Emerson's secret, I venture, was his casualness with this as with his other poems. "Toy with the bow," he said elsewhere, "but hit the white." He did not tear his hair over a poem as Lowell did over his "Commemoration Ode." When "Concord Hymn" was sung to the tune of "Old Hundred" by a band of youths and maidens at the completion of the Battle Monument in Concord on July 4, 1837, Emerson was not even present. He was away visiting in Plymouth.

Nowhere in his fourteen-volume journal or in any of his six volumes of letters, so far as I can find out, did he mention the poem. It was mentioned by his mother in a letter to her son William.

Had Emerson been asked by his fellow townsmen to write something for the occasion? Or had he himself taken the initiative and offered his services? Whichever the case, the poem, like most occasional poems, was doubly occasional, written both for and about the occasion.

Now the chief trouble with writing for and about an occasion is that you become so impressed with the importance of the occasion that you are likely to become impressed with the importance of your writing about it. Something big, obviously, is called for.

One thing, aside from his good taste, that helped save Emerson from bigness was the fact that the poem would be sung to a simple hymn tune. Though "Old Hundred," in the singing, must have weighed down Emerson's winged words, in the writing the old tune probably served at least to keep the poem lean.

Production Belt

A poem comes onto the moving belt sometimes as a piece of paper with a few words scribbled on it, but many a poem begins its journey less tangibly as a mere hint, a hunch, a possibility, and may travel for considerable time and distance before pen, pencil, or typewriter comes into operation.

During overt composition a poem may travel a surprisingly short or long time and distance. Yet when "finished," its travel along the belt may have hardly more than begun. The marketing phase begins. And this too may take the poem a short or long time and distance.

If it is accepted for magazine publication, it goes on moving patiently along the belt, unable to do much of anything except to be patient, until the magazine comes out. A small flurry of activity may accompany this event; the arrival of a check, its cashing, and the paying of one or two small bills.

Still the poem rides on. In due course it becomes one in a book of poems and, if accepted by a publisher, enters a phase of bustling and varied activity on the belt. After publication activity continues though spottily—the arrival of reviews, requests to reprint, and invitations to the author to give poetry readings. Also from time to time there may arrive a small check.

Of course a poem may be thrown off the belt or fall off at any point. We are assuming that this poem stays on for as long a ride as possible. Further transformations await it, such as its reappearance in a volume called *Selected Poems*, and later in a volume called *Collected Poems*. Even this is not the end.

Having followed one poem in its long journey, we

might look at the whole belt with many poems riding on it in various stages of progress. During a typical day the poet will be at work now at one location along the belt and now at another. Poem *A* he may be sending to a magazine, poem *B* may be still in the polishing and testing stage, poem *C* he has not finished writing, and poem *D* is a gleam in his eye.

He is at his best when he has poems well spaced along the belt, and it does him good to move from one working position to another. To have poems past and poems future, poems coming and poems going, is to feel confident, secure, and full of life. A hitch anywhere along the line can interfere with progress everywhere else. If and when the belt slows down and stops moving, poets have been known to do desperate things. But as long as the belt moves and there are poems to the right of him and poems to the left of him, the poet has no trouble keeping busy. He has a full-time job.

Labels

They wrote to ask what label I wanted under my picture. I looked at my three predecessors of the previous year. One was "Poet, teacher, and editor." The second was "Poet, teacher, and literary critic." The third was "Poet, poetry anthologist, and editor."

Why were poets, I asked myself, never satisfied to be poets? Why were they always something else and something else? As if a poet had to have three persons to be on firm ground?

What label did I want? "Poet." Nothing more.

Of course, there were all sorts of other labels I could have added. "Property owner, taxpayer, car driver, typist, letter writer, book reader, traveler, gardener." But I suspected that the more other things I was the less poet I might be. Besides, long after I had stopped traveling and paying taxes I might still, God willing, be a poet.

So I said, "Poet." Period.

A bit bold, perhaps, for one who when he began to be a poet didn't want to be called one. Before my first volume I avoided the label whenever I could. If people called me poet seriously, I didn't deserve it. If not seriously, I preferred not to be a stock joke. But that was long ago.

"Poet," I said.

When the publication appeared, I looked to find myself. There was my picture all right, but under it this label: "Lecturer, critic, teacher, poet."

Somebody—Nobody

Somebody, hearing that Emily had called herself a Nobody, decided to be a Nobody too—not just any Nobody
but a Nobody who really was a Somebody, like Emily.

Santayana, Columbus, and
Samuel Eliot Morison

Though poets have long been hailed as Truth-Speakers, their reputation as liars has been no less persistent. Isn't it precisely when a poet draws breath to utter a Truth that he is most in danger of lying?

Take Santayana. In his celebrated sonnet he says of Columbus, "To trust the soul's invincible surmise / Was all his science and his only art."

This statement is not only untrue, it is less than flattering to Columbus. Had not Columbus been a shrewd, experienced seaman using every scrap of scientific knowledge available and every trick of the navigator's art, he never would have reached America. If you have any doubts of this, I refer you to another Harvard professor who wrote about Columbus, Samuel Eliot Morison.

That Columbus had a soul I do not question, or that his soul had a surmise or that the surmise was invincible. I insist only that soul was not the whole story.

Today a poet has perhaps a better chance of speaking the truth than poets had in Santayana's day, Truth-Speaking in poetry having largely gone out of fashion.

The Pathetic Fallacy

It sounds like something nobody would wish to be guilty of. Who wants to be fallacious? Who wants to be pathetic?

This unhappy phrase was coined by Ruskin. Though he does his best to make clear that the pathetic fallacy is all right in its place and may even be very beautiful and moving, his best is not good enough. A readiness to form categories and make judgments does not altogether conceal the confusion in his thought. The more he particularizes and qualifies the more we too become confused. Indeed he gives us more fallacies than the one he gives a name to.

According to Ruskin, when a poet misrepresents the outer world or distorts what we are pleased to call reality, he may be moved either (1) by "wilful fancy," or (2) "by an excited state of the feelings making him, for the time, more or less irrational." It is the second fallacy that Ruskin calls "pathetic."

But having drawn this distinction, he proceeds to muddy the waters. Here is his illustration of fallacy number one, and here also is one of his illustrations of fallacy number two, the pathetic. The reader might amuse himself by trying to tell which is which.

> The spendthrift crocus, bursting through the
>   mould
> Naked and shivering, with his cup of gold.
>   [O. W. Holmes]

> The one red leaf, the last of its clan,
> That dances as often as dance it can.
>   [Coleridge]

Another illustration he gives of the pathetic fallacy is this:

> They rowed her in across the rolling foam—
> The cruel, crawling foam.
>
> [Kingsley]

This is a clearer case, granted, but even here we want to ask questions. Is the voice that speaks in these lines irrational or morbid? Are the men who row the drowned girl home irrational or morbid? The evidence is that they are not. Grief-stricken they may be and grim, but perfectly lucid. They know the sea. They know the sea can drown. They have encountered this thing before. How can they have any illusion? If the sea is cruel as a cat or snake, it is cruel not because it is imagined to be a cat or snake but because it is the sea.

The voice speaking in these lines is not only lucid but calm. The rowers go on with their grim task. There is no fallacy here at all.

What Ruskin calls falsification or distortion is best interpreted neither as wilful fancy nor as unhinged reason, but as the poet's central desire to find a language powerful enough to match his vision.

Ruskin's chief interest in the pathetic fallacy seems to be his claim that only poets of the second order indulge in it freely. Poets of the first order—Homer and Dante— are strong enough to get along without it, indeed are all the stronger for getting along without it.

Later on we are told that the pathetic fallacy is characteristic of modern poets and painters. The ancient and medieval mind was unfriendly to it. So, after building up his case for poets of the first order, he pulls it down. Homer avoided the pathetic fallacy not because he was a poet of the first order but because he lived in an age when everybody else felt and did the same. Likewise with Dante.

Ruskin cites with enthusiasm one modern poem that avoids the fallacy. Is it by a poet of the first order? Casimir de la Vigne in his poem "La Toilette de Constance."

Poor pathetic fallacy.

The Man Who Wrote One Poem

It was an enviable position he was in. He could be a poet or not a poet according to mood and company. He could say yes or no and prove it.

If somebody said to him, "But you write poetry, don't you?" he could say, "Actually I've written just one poem in my life, and one swallow doesn't make a summer."

At another time in another mood he could, if he wished, murmur casually, "That reminds me of a little poem I once wrote." He wouldn't have to say it was his only one.

Of course he knew his poem by heart. It was instantly available.

Should anybody be so ungracious as to look down his nose at the little poem, the author could always defend himself with, "But what do you expect of a *first* poem?"

Presumably he could have gone on writing other poems like other poets. But he knew when to stop. Having proved that he could do it, he had the sense not to go on repeating himself.

Enviable chap.

Dame Edith

If poetry really needs something extra and special, some flash of color, some dramatic heightening, then, better than all the prizes and gold medals and fancy dinners and White House flourishes, would it be to persuade Dame Edith Sitwell to return from the realm of shades. To see her once again regally or ecclesiastically robed and seated in a great chair made to simulate a throne, looking like Elizabeth the First or Lady Macbeth or Robert Graves's portrait of the White Goddess.

And should she find her audience annoying, to hear again her voice lifted in denunciation. To hear again perchance what she is reported once to have told an Edinburgh audience:

"No one has ever been more alive than I am. I am an electric eel in a pond full of flatfish."

Duty

Strange things poets sometimes say, and not in our own day only. Wordsworth, for instance, beginning his "Ode to Duty," addresses her as "Stern daughter of the voice of God."

Now a daughter of God is something we can grasp, but what are we to make of a daughter of the voice of God?

One would suppose that the voice of God itself would serve very well as Duty. Wordsworth, however, obviously wanted something feminine to apostrophize, something like the Muse if not the Muse herself. Yet if he had called Duty the daughter of God, he would have got himself into theological hot water. For God to have a Son is of the very essence of things; but for God to have a Daughter would smack of paganism.

The Greeks were realistic. Every goddess or demi-goddess had both father and mother. The Muses were daughters of Zeus and Mnemosyne (Memory). Our cherubim and seraphim, on the other hand, and all the orders of the angelic host are asexual or epicene. Though the angels have masculine names, in Christmas pageantry their roles are unhesitatingly taken by high-school girls in white cheesecloth and flowing hair. Wordsworth's solution was theologically safe, and as poetry it has passed muster these many years.

Long ago when Wordsworth was my favorite poet and I knew the "Ode to Duty" by heart, I never once questioned the parentage he gave her. If in those days a skeptic had raised his eyebrows, I would doubtless have defended Wordsworth by saying that poetry was not meant to make sense but to lift up the heart.

Today few odes are written, and very very few to Duty. Indeed, the very word Duty is heard on our lips how seldom, how seldom.

Poetry as an Un-American Activity

If the notion ever got around that poetry was an un-American activity (as in some respects it certainly is) and that poets were dangerous people (as some of them surely have been and are), and if instead of being encouraged with prizes, awards, gold medals, fellowships, and other subsidies, they were penalized and even suppressed—

So that to escape fines and prison sentences and loss of good name and employment as college teachers, most poets stopped writing poetry altogether—

Except when, on very rare occasions, a poem so insisted on being written that the poet yielded to temptation despite all risks and wrote a poem he was willing to die for—

If, in other words, poetry almost disappeared from the earth and only occasionally in some out-of-the-way place bubbled up like a pure mountain spring—

Too Busy for Both

If it is true that not everyone who goes to a poetry reading is invited to the party afterward, it is equally true that not everyone at the party has been to the reading. People too busy for both poetry and drinks tend to prefer the latter. At one stroke they escape both the poetry and the obligation to say something pleasant about it.

They remind me of those insects—bumblebees, I believe—who instead of working their way down into a flower for its nectar, sometimes cut a hole at the base of the blossom and so get their nectar the easy way. Though botanists disapprove the practice, I cannot find it in my heart to condemn it.

The Messy Muse

"You see," my friend said the other day, "you're not really a poet at all."

He paused for my reaction. Finding me receptive, he proceeded.

"To begin with, you're too orderly. Poetry is not so much order as disorder. A sweet disorder, to use Herrick's phrase, though I grant that today the disorder is more often bitter or sour than sweet. Poetry is actually a blend of order and disorder. You—you're just order and nothing else. The muse of poetry is the Unconscious and she is notably messy."

Was there the slightest possible smile on his lips? Or was their curve noncommittal? Even I who knew that expression so well could not be sure.

"In the second place, you're too sane. Lovers, madmen, and poets—wasn't it Plato who pointed out their kinship? Even if a poet can't manage to be mad, he should at least have his ups and downs. If you ever had any ups and downs, I never noticed them."

His candor held me spellbound.

"In the third place, you're not a rebel. You're not against things—the universe or society or the administration. You never learned to rage. I'll be damned if you ever even wanted to learn. You're too philosophic. You were born to be a philosopher, and got sidetracked somewhere along the line into poetry."

"I see," I said.

"Of course," he concluded, "I don't deny, I'd be the last person in the world to want to deny, that you've turned out some rather remarkable poems."

Mr. Eliot's Cats

When T. S. Eliot assembled the volume called *The Complete Poems and Plays of T. S. Eliot,* he placed between *Murder in the Cathedral* and *The Four Quartets, Old Possum's Book of Practical Cats.*

How comes it that I never heard or read any comment on this extraordinary juxtaposition?

Between his greatest play and his last great lyric achievement, precisely here we have "Old Deuteronomy" and the others.

Was this Eliot's humor? Or was it his humility? Or both?

He might, of course, have omitted "Old Possum" from *The Complete Poems and Plays* altogether. Or, including it, he might have put it at the end, perhaps in smaller type. Instead he put it where he did. Evidently the assembling of his collected poems was not an ordeal for Mr. Eliot.

When we take a writer very Seriously, Seriously with a capital S, we run the risk of taking him more Seriously than he takes himself. One recalls Max Beerbohm's little Mary Augusta (later, much later, Mrs. Humphry Ward) in red ruffled dress, with hands folded demurely behind her, looking up at her uncle, Matthew Arnold, towering above her with an enormous grin on his face, and saying:

"Why, Uncle Matthew, Oh why, will not you be always wholly serious?"

Noncriticism

Scornful of nonpersons, e e cummings was happy writing his nonpoems and giving his nonlectures.

Presumably he felt that a person ought to be a person and failed when he was something else, whereas a poem ought to be something else and failed when it was a poem.

Wild but Polished

For these exhilarating words we are indebted to the jazz pianist, Dorothy Donegan, and to *Time* magazine which on November 3, 1958, published a brief interview with her.

Even without the accompanying photo (caught obviously in a wild moment) it would be easy to picture her. A little toss of the head, "I'm wild." Then another toss, "But I'm polished." She was speaking, of course, of her piano playing. But what wouldn't a poet, any poet, give to be able to say the same of his poetry?

Miss Donegan didn't say she combined freedom and form. She is not a lady professor. She took the extreme of freedom, wildness, and the extreme of form, polish, and let the two strike sparks.

The American word "wild" is full of wonderful ambiguities. A wild boxer or baseball pitcher is no good, but the ski coach who called a certain youth "a wild man on skis" meant only praise. "Wild" is lack of control, and "wild" is such virtuoso control that the wild man can take beautiful chances. No one will misunderstand Miss Donegan.

Even within the good kind of wildness there are differences. There is the leaping, soaring wildness of a wild animal or bird; there is also the perfectly quiet wildness of wild fruit whose most notable distinguishing feature is flavor. Some wild poems are deer or hawks. Others are wild strawberries in the grass, wild apples in the woods.

This is not to say the wilder the better. Can a poem be too wild? This depends partly on your taste: you may prefer only a trace of wildness, wildness as a trace element. It also depends on what you mean by wildness. If a poem is so wildly leaping that it leaps permanently beyond your grasp, that is one thing. But flavor is another thing and it is hard to see how a poem can have too much.

Can a poem be too polished? This also depends on your taste and also on what you are polishing. Contrary to what is often said, polishing doesn't always result in polishing away. Are you polishing a piece of chalk or a diamond?

If you are only wild or only polished, you face the danger of too much. But if, like Dorothy Donegan, you are both wild and polished, you are fairly safe and very good.

The poetry we call modern has been no more polished than the poetry that preceded it (and sometimes distinctly less so), but no one can deny that it has been wilder with every sort of wildness.

Goddess

Robert Graves, in his celebrated book, pictures the White Goddess as a bloodsucking vampire luring men to destruction. Mr. Graves's unqualified devotion to the Goddess cannot be other than touching. His devotion, indeed, is like that of the male spider fated to be consumed by the female immediately after the act of love. Since the female is often overeager to begin before the male has finished, he offers her a small insect wrapped in a veil to appease her appetite for the moment and divert her attention.

Some scholars have questioned the existence of the White Goddess. I fear she is all too real.

Advantages in Being a Poet

It is the disadvantages, of course, that we hear most about today—the dwindling audience, the swelling publication costs, and so forth. Yet there are still advantages in being a poet.

Take security, for instance. Who has more? If he has put the best of himself into his poems, then the best of himself is to a large degree safe. He is safe not only because what he most wants to keep safe is in his poems, but also because the poems themselves are compact enough to be kept safely. Unpublished they can be filed in a fireproof cabinet or vault. Published in book form they have the greater safety of wide distribution in libraries. Compare this situation with a painter's eternal problem of where to keep his unsold paintings safely, accessibly, and not too expensively.

The days drift by. The poet writes a small poem. And then another poem. They add up. They become a small volume. Then another volume. The volumes add up. *Selected Poems,* perhaps, and possibly *Collected Poems.* The poet is now an old man with one book containing his life.

Or suppose he never has a volume published. In some safe place, as safe as possible, he keeps a loose-leaf notebook containing, neatly typed, all his poems that have stood the test of nonpublication.

A second enviable advantage a poet has is his freedom to work on a poem almost anywhere he happens to be—train, bus, plane, waiting room, park bench, bed. Since an impulse may strike unexpectedly and does so more often than not, he is lucky to need only the common pencil in his pocket and a piece of paper. Even if he is dependent on a typewriter, a pencil will do to sketch a poem or revise one already down on paper. Nobody around him need know what he is doing. He might be a traveling salesman figuring his accounts.

Odd times and places are not only possible for poetry, they may actually spur it. Jet travel can be very favorable, thanks to the freedom from interruption, the steadiness of the plane, the sense of being on top of things, and the powerful hum that blots out lesser noises. A painter or composer in flight might sketch a figure or a theme; the poet can do the whole poem.

Another advantage, though one that some poets might not admit, is the willingness of people to make allowances for him just because he is a poet. He is not required to know anything in particular. He is not supposed to be efficient like other men. Social position with him, if he has any, does not depend on possessions. If he looks a little shabby, why not? He is a poet. He may drive an old car with dignity. He may even walk. In short, he may be comfortable, if he is willing. And being comfortable and noncompetitive (except in his poetry, of course) he has little or nothing to come between himself and the writing of his next poem.

No Poem So Fine

No poem is so fine that some critic can't damn it if he has a mind to. Poetry, unlike light verse which plays safe and does all the laughing without getting laughed at, is defenseless, takes all the risks, goes out on a limb, sometimes very far out. The more a poem is a poem the closer it plays to the absurd, trusting the reader to tell the difference.

No poem is fine enough to be safe. A critic can always maul it or pooh-pooh it if he has a mind to. Poems have not learned jujitsu or karate. They go naked and trusting.

On the other hand, no poem is too wretched for some critic (if he has a mind to) to hail as a gem.

Woman with the Tape Recorder

She arrives with a pleasant bustle, the woman with the tape recorder. She has taped so-and-so and so-and-so and so-and-so, all of them my betters. Now she has come to tape me. Is she doing me a favor? Not exactly. At least she doesn't seem to imply that she is. Am I doing her a favor? Not exactly either. Her manner does not suggest that I am. It is simply that poets these days are being taped, taped as unprotestingly and unceremoniously as maples in sap season are tapped.

Unlike poems in print which are protected by copyright and contract, poems on tape enjoy a large freedom. They may be played by the possessor to a live audience, or played over the air to a larger audience, or played intimately in the boudoir, or played not at all. The tape recorder captures not only the poet's poems but the poet's voice as well. When the woman with the tape recorder leaves, it may seem that she has just about captured the poet himself.

This time, however, things turned out a bit differently. Taper and poet got to talking pleasantly about one thing and another until it was time for her to go. The poet remained untaped, untapped.

Emily and I

The year that Emily Dickinson was born (1830), my father's father, Daniel, was a lusty young man of twenty who in that very year left Ireland for America by sailing ship. When Emily was fifteen, Daniel entered the Harvard Medical School from which he graduated two years later. When Daniel died in 1867, after twenty strenuous years as a country doctor in Nova Scotia, Emily was at the peak of her poetic power or a little beyond, and my father was one year old. When Emily died in 1886, my father was a lusty young man of twenty, and I was born fifteen years later.

Silent Poetry

The idea of silent poetry or silence in poetry used to puzzle as well as fascinate me. I wanted such poetry to exist but I couldn't quite see how if by "silent" was meant "wordless" or "nonspeaking."

Recently it has occurred to me that a silent poem may be like a silent man. By a silent man we ordinarily mean not one who doesn't speak at all but one who speaks little. Little enough to impress us with his nonspeaking. Why couldn't a silent poem similarly mean one that impresses us with what it leaves unsaid? A poem not only less talkative than most prose but less talkative than much poetry?

Silent people are usually silent by nature. Silent poems have to achieve their silence. It is possible that a silent person may say little simply because he has little to say. The silence of a silent poem is pregnant.

A poem benefits doubly by its component of silence. The silence itself is delightful and at the same time provides the perfect foil for what is spoken. A silent poem comes to us on a white background.

How is silence achieved? A very short poem, like a cry on a still night, makes the surrounding stillness more vivid by breaking it. A longer poem may have somewhat the same quality if it seems to be made up of very short poems, that is, has a fragmentary character. Or if transitions and connections are omitted. All clean prose has a degree of silence; but poetry may begin where prose leaves off, omitting not only all unnecessary words but even some words that might be thought necessary.

A poem that presents an object or scene or situation without comment approaches the silence of painting or sculpture. Any formality is silent since it contrasts with mere noise and chatter. Yet the very casual can be silent too, if its manner is one of musing rather than of talking. Ultimately silence in poetry depends on restraint and control. The more a poem has of either or both the more silent it is.

If you say that all poets love words, you might add that some poets love words so completely they trust them to the limit, while other poets love words no less but distrust them a little. The latter are the silent poets.

The word-trusting poet may be charmingly exuberant. He may be Irish. I am far from ready to say that only silent poems are fine poems.

Like a silent person a silent poem stands aside. Stands aside from chatter and chance conversation. Stands aside from all shouting. Stands aside also from artiness and calculated effect which we call rhetoric. Stands aside even from song, for song is even less silent than speech, the singing voice sounding continuously whereas the speaking voice is broken by innumerable minute silences.

Since the general tone of poetry in our century has shifted from singing to speaking, we may all of us have been moving one degree nearer silent poetry.

Hard

When Robert Frost said he liked poems hard he could scarcely have meant he liked them difficult. If he had meant difficult he would have said he didn't like them easy. What he said was that he didn't like them soft.

Poems can be soft in several ways. They can be soft in form (invertebrate). They can be soft in thought and feeling (sentimental). They can be soft with excess verbiage. Frost used to advise one to squeeze the water out of a poem. He liked poems dry. What is dry tends to be hard, and what is hard is always dry, except perhaps on the outside.

Yet though hardness here does not mean difficulty, some difficulty naturally goes with hardness. A hard poem may not be hard to read but it is hard to write. Not too hard, preferably. Not so hard to write that there is no flow in the writer. But hard enough for the growing poem to meet with some healthy resistance. Frost often found this healthy resistance in a tight rhyme scheme and strict meter. There are other ways of getting good resistance, of course.

And in the reader too, a hard poem will bring some difficulty. Preferably not too much. Not enough difficulty to completely baffle him. Ideally a hard poem should not be too hard to make sense of, but hard to exhaust its meaning and its beauty.

"What I care about is the hardness of the poems. I don't like them soft, I want them to be little pebbles, but placed where they won't dislodge easily. And I'd like them to be little pebbles of precious stone—precious, or semiprecious." (Interview with John Ciardi, *Saturday Review,* March 21, 1959.)

Here is hard prose talking about hard poetry. Frost was never shrewder or more illuminating. Here, as well as in anything else he ever said, is his flavor.

What contemporary of his can you imagine saying this or anything like it?

In 1843 Emerson jotted in his journal: "Hard clouds and hard expressions, and hard manners, I love."

Poetry as Stuff

Recently an Ohio woman, a stranger to me, wrote to ask a favor, and graciously ended her letter with the remark: "I love your stuff."

I had almost forgotten the word, and how, long ago, one young poet would say to another: "I'll show you my stuff." Much as a boy might say to another: "I'll show you my marbles if you'll show me yourn."

As a synonym for poetry "stuff" doubtless has its virtues. It is down-to-earth, tough, and utterly unpretentious. When you call your own poetry stuff, you aren't making any claims for it. It may be awful. Or it may be rather good. You aren't saying. Let others say.

On the other hand, when you call somebody else's poetry stuff, you aren't implying or insinuating anything. It may be damn fine stuff indeed.

Yet somehow I never could bring myself to use the expression. Stuff? Stuff was precisely what my own poems were not. To other people, perhaps, but not to me. If sometimes other people's poetry seemed to me no better than stuff, that, of course, was all the more reason for not using the word.

No, no. And yet—to be perfectly honest with myself— while I've been talking about it, I wonder if I haven't been growing a little fond of the word after all?

Lowell

"Weak-winged is song," sang Lowell at the commencement of his "Commemoration Ode." At this point he may have given thanks to have made so promising a start, for the ode, as he himself tells us, was proving one big headache.

But though the words ring out, do they speak the truth? Song may be ever so weak in everything else, weak-headed and weak-handed, weak-kneed and weak-footed, but surely not weak-winged. Wings are what song is strong in. Yes. Wings make song song, make song sing.

Poor Lowell! And after all his labor!

Poet on the Platform

A song composer doesn't sing his songs in public unless he is also a singer. A poet reads his poems in public as a matter of course.

To sing well enough to sing in public is acknowledged to be an art requiring both aptitude and training. Is it an art to read one's poems in public?

The answer varies. Yes. No. Yes and no. It varies according to who is answering the question. It also varies according to the poet who is reading.

Those who say, "No, the reading of poetry aloud is not an art," may add, "unfortunately." Or they may add, "Thank God." Poetry reading, according to a prevailing sentiment, is not only not an art, it had better not try to be. Let it keep as far as possible from art, artifice, artiness, artificiality, and every other nonsense. The poet is asked to be natural, nothing less and nothing more. If he stutters, well then let him stutter. If he lisps, let him be true to his lisping. Let him stand before us as God made him.

The poems he has written may or may not be art. He himself may regard them as art or as nonart. They may be extremely artistic or extremely inartistic. But when he reads them to us or speaks them for us, let the words come from his lips as effortlessly and artlessly as leaves coming out on a tree.

With fundamental and unmistakable honesty he stands before us, asking us nothing, promising us nothing. "Just as I am without one plea."

We who have come to hear him may or may not be able to hear. If we hear, may or may not understand. If we understand, may or may not enjoy.

He stands before us as God made him, stark naked, yet curiously unembarrassed. Nor are we who have come to hear him particularly embarrassed either.

Anyone not wholly content with this situation, anyone dreaming of a poet's voice presenting poems with the clearness with which picture glass presents pictures, can comfort himself with the thought that though the situation may not be ideal it might easily be worse. If the poet whom God made took it into his head to remake himself a little, to improve his reading, the result would not necessarily and invariably be improvement. Perhaps it is awareness of this misfortune that makes an audience prefer to risk a poet reading without art rather than with. The faults for which God is responsible are easier to forgive than those for which the poet himself is exclusively to blame.

Redress of Grievance

Something a friend told me long ago keeps bothering me a little. Among the reviews of his first book of poems was one especially unfriendly. It wasn't so much that the reviewer condemned the book as that he seemed determined to condemn it. What he said was imperceptive as well as hostile. Could he have even read the book?

A few years later reviewer and author found themselves together at the MacDowell Colony. The reviewer was in a friendly mood. He asked the poet to forgive him for his review, explaining that he had written it to vent a grudge scarcely related to the book at all.

An interesting point. Is private apology due restitution for public wrong?

If a reviewer has simply changed his mind about a book, he may want to say so in print when he has a chance, and this in fairness both to the book and to himself. Whether he condemned a book too harshly or praised it too lavishly, he might welcome any suitable occasion for setting the record straight. But he would hardly be under any obligation to do this. All of us are changing our minds about everything all the time. Having set a record straight, we might have to keep on indefinitely.

What bothers me is not a mistaken judgment but a miscarriage of justice. What does the Bill of Rights say about this? What are a poem's civil liberties under the Constitution?

To Dislike Poetry
Is Not Necessarily to Disparage It

Isn't it naive to assume that what makes a fine poem necessarily makes enjoyable reading? Intensity, honesty, articulateness? Who doesn't have among his acquaintances an intense, honest, and articulate person whose visits one would be happy to be spared? Emerson once observed that people should be taken in small doses. Much poetry today gives us the poet himself or herself in massive doses.

One might read poetry as one takes a good medicine, a good bad-tasting medicine, as a stimulant, perhaps, or as a purgative. But having taken a few doses, one may not wish or need to take more.

To dislike poetry is not always a confession of inability to understand it. Some poems, some fine poems, like some fine people, one might dislike all the more the better one got to know them.

Chaos

"There is simply not enough chaos in his soul," says the *Irish Times* reviewer of a certain Irish poet.

Closing my eyes I can imagine he is talking about me, chaos being something I too am weak in.

What can a poet do, what can he hope to achieve, in whose soul chaos is deficient?

First Person Singular

After all the innovations and inundations and revolutions in poetry in our century, the breaking down and sweeping away of what had long been thought the foundations, the boundless liberty that poets including the most esteemed, indeed the most esteemed most of all, have helped themselves to and reveled in, the all-inclusive and now unchallenged liberty to write anything one pleases in any way he pleases—it seems hardly possible that anyone however isolated and superannuated could ask such a question.

"Do you consider it permissible to use the first person singular pronoun in a poem?"

Yet it was not a seventeen-year locust just out of the ground who asked, but a woman without exception the most serious looking I ever saw. She wore pinch-on glasses which seemed to defy anyone or anything to dislodge them, and through the glasses she looked at me with a seriousness that verged on fury.

"Do you consider it permissible to use the first person singular pronoun in a poem?"

Suddenly I felt light-headed. I wanted to mount a table and do a dance. But I restrained myself. The serious woman was asking a perfectly serious question which she had probably asked in other classes, workshops, and clubs where the answer had been sometimes yes and sometimes no. She was merely sounding me out in order to fit me into her framework.

I've regretted ever since that I didn't give her a really thorough answer.

"No, I do not regard it as permissible. And I mean of course not only 'I' but 'my' and 'mine' and 'me.' And 'we,' 'our,' and 'us' too. It may surprise you but I do feel it is wiser to omit the second person pronoun as well, both singular and plural."

Then by delicate steps I would have worked up to the point of omitting the third person. Then all pronouns, then nouns. And I could have hinted at still more drastic restrictions.

I see her now as she looked at me through those glasses. Even her gray hair was seriously arranged.

"Do you consider it permissible—?"

Poet as Noble Achievement

In an address at Amherst College in 1959, the distinguished historian, Henry Steele Commager, remarked: "What Amherst student does not know that to be a poet is the noblest achievement of man?"

This brings up the old conundrum: When is a poet a poet and when is a poet not a poet?

When is a poet a poet and when is a poet merely someone who writes poetry? Where lies the dividing line?

If you say that someone who writes poetry but is not a poet doesn't really write poetry at all but rather something else or something less than poetry, something sometimes called "verse," then the question shifts to another. When is poetry poetry and when is poetry not poetry?

But even if we could agree on what poetry is when it really is poetry, would we be willing to agree that everyone who writes it is a poet? A poet, that is, who really is a poet?

Surely Dr. Commager does not mean that each and every writer of poetry or of what passes as poetry is the noblest achievement of man.

If you asked him to name a poet who is the noblest achievement of man, he might name Shakespeare.

That Shakespeare was himself a noble achievement and made a noble achievement no one will deny. But was he any nobler and did he do any more nobly than Michelangelo? Or Johann Sebastian Bach?

Is even the noblest poet any nobler than the noblest philosopher or saint or schoolteacher or historian or carpenter? A *really* noble carpenter? And I mean not just a carpenter who does carpentry however fine, but a carpenter who is a carpenter.

Vacations

Punctually each June the *New Yorker* notifies me that during July and August their poetry department will be closed. "Only topical light verse or poems scheduled for imminent book publication should be submitted during this period."

I wish I knew whether any of their other departments close during the summer and go on vacation. If the poetry department is the only one to shut down, I wish I knew why.

Strange that this should be the first year I have asked these questions or paid much attention to the *New Yorker*'s thoughtful annual warning. Perhaps it is because this year I am trying so desperately to get my own poetry department going once again.

The Disillusioning Blurb

A poet has all the poems in his book to prove himself a poet. But the blurb writer has the last word. On the back flap of the dust jacket he can reduce the poet to a brief paragraph of bald prose.

He tells us that the poet was born, and, what is worse, when and where. To be born is bad enough, but to be born, say, in Binghamton and in 1906! Even if such information be not wholly irrelevant, it imposes severe limitations on the imagination.

If there is any truth in the saying that poets are born and not made, it is the truth of a second birth. When a poet is truly born, it is a considerable number of years after he was born a squalling baby. Of the baby we can say 1906; but is there any date for the poet?

Blurb writers seem to have no inkling of this. How seldom it is that one encounters a blurb writer worthy of being trusted with the back flap of the poet's dust jacket. How seldom one ever comes across anything that approaches the adequate. "The author of these poems was suckled by a she-wolf, weened on locusts and wild honey, and is married to seven goddesses."

A Golden Simplicity?

Have you never noticed how perfectly still some poems lie on the printed page? As the reader's eye brushes over them, as the mind flits across them, they never stir.

This is not to say that they may not be fine poems, well worth an acquaintance. But the reader must wake them up before he can make that acquaintance. The reader must take the initiative.

Perhaps you are glancing through a new anthology not so much to find something to read as just to see what is there. Page after page, poem after poem, until your heart, in spite of you, grows hardened. The more pages you turn the more convinced, yea the more determined, you are that no poem will give you pleasure. Your heart has hardened indeed.

Page after page, poem after poem. Did any of them really want to be written, and not just submit to a poet who wanted to write them? Did all of them really want to be written by a poet?

Page after—then something happens. Something you had forgotten was possible. Your eye is caught by something in the poem before you, some slight movement or the hint of it. And before you know it the poem of its own accord rises from the page and comes toward you!

That day it may well be you turn no more pages.

Later, thinking back, you wonder just what it was about that poem that made it rise from the white page and come toward you. It may be forever impossible to say. A breath of air circulating among the words? A golden simplicity? An arresting candor?

Required Reading

"These are among the truly miraculous works of our time, and ought to be required reading for every beginning poet."

How strangely, how unaccountably, the second part of this sentence follows the first. Miracles, one might suppose, would be sufficiently observed without being required.

But if the reviewer really means what he says, will he kindly tell us what Authority or Establishment, what Academy or Benevolent Despot, would pass such a law?

Furthermore, if this miraculous book is to be made required reading, surely other miraculous books of poetry should be treated likewise—the plays of Shakespeare, for instance, and the *Divine Comedy*. What would be the complete curriculum of required reading for a beginning poet?

By "required reading" I assume the reviewer does not mean actual compulsion. If the beginning poet refused or failed to do his reading, he would be penalized, but no overt force would necessarily be brought to bear.

Professional Poet

Someone the other day called me a professional poet to my face.

"Don't call me that," I cried. "Don't call anybody that. As well talk about a professional friend."

"Oh!" he said.

"Or a professional lover."

"Oh!"

Poetry and Poverty

In his anthology, *The Pleasures of Poverty,* Anthony Bertram makes clear that it is not destitution he is praising. Only a saint can flourish on nothing. But anybody can flourish on enough and no more if he wants to.

The poems and prose selections in his anthology demonstrate that many writers of the past have thought of poverty as something positive. When they praise it, what they are really praising is a very modest, sometimes a ridiculously modest, wealth. Herrick, for instance:

> Here, here I live with what my board
> Can with the smallest cost afford.
> Though n'er so mean the viands be,
> They well content my Prue and me.
> Or pea, or bean, or wort, or beet,
> Whatever comes, content makes sweet.

Today this sort of poverty is not only out of fashion, it is out of mind and perhaps out of existence except in very out-of-the-way places. Today when a man is poor he is poor. He is substandard. And it is not an occasion for congratulation, his own or anybody else's. Robert Herrick's contentment of three centuries ago would be called by another name today.

Yet even so, Herrick may be not altogether irrelevant to us. A young poet just out of college and not yet married might consider a Herrick sort of life for a few years. With a small income, preferably from part-time work, he could be both comfortable and independent. Like Herrick he could grow the pea, the bean, the wort, the beet, and like Herrick he could keep a hen. Rough clothes, old clothes, would be fine. A good half the day or half the year he could have clear for himself and poetry.

Even if he didn't wholly like such a life, it might be better than going hungry in New York or Paris. He could always move to the city whenever his income permitted. And while living in the country he wouldn't be obliged to write poems in praise of it or in praise of his poverty.

He might, of course, like it. He might decide to stay on. Healthy, solvent, and independent, he might find cottage life good for him, and being good for him good for his poetry as well.

The Indecipherable Poem

I have no love for the indecipherable poem, but for the indecipherable poet I have often a warm friendly feeling. He is usually a bright chap, perhaps brilliant, a good talker, someone worth knowing and worth watching. He is also often a college undergraduate majoring in English and in love with writing.

In his literature and writing courses it is taken for granted that the significant poets are the difficult ones. So, what less can an undergraduate poet do than be difficult himself?

Difficulty, of course, is not the only virtue of great poets. They give us passion, vision, originality. None of these the undergraduate poet probably has, but he *can* be difficult. He can be as difficult as he wants to be. He can be as difficult as anybody else. He need only give the words he uses a private set of meanings. It is not difficult to be difficult.

What I mean is, a poem that is very difficult to read may not have been at all difficult to write.

One poem sufficiently difficult can keep a creative writing class busy a whole hour. If its young author feels pleased with himself, can we blame him? He is human. He has produced something as difficult as anything by Ezra Pound. Why shouldn't he be pleased?

If he wants to, he can let his classmates pick away at his poem indefinitely and never set them straight. If his teacher ventures to criticize a phrase or a line, the author can say that the passage is exactly as he wants it. Is it awkward? Well, he intended it to be awkward since awkwardness was needed at that point. This would be clear, he murmurs, to anyone who understood the poem.

Nobody can touch him. Nobody at all. He is safe. In an ever-threatening world full of old perils and new, such security is to be envied. To be able to sit tight and pretty on top of your poem, impregnable like a little castle perched on a steep rock.

Electronically Equipped

For some years now I have been intending to have myself electronically equipped for prompt criticism of poems. A card of certain dimensions bearing the poem clearly typed could be deposited in one pocket. Then, after the pushing of a button, another card bearing the criticism would be found in a pocket on the opposite side.

There would be a special button to push for any poet who wanted to make a comment on his poem, such as: "This just came to me. I haven't changed a word."

There would be another button to push for any poet who wanted to ask a specific question, such as: "Should I keep on writing?"

And of course there would be a special pocket from which coins could be recovered if anything had gone amiss with the mechanism.

The Satirical Rogue

I asked the Irish poet if he would be surprised to hear that I was one-quarter Irish myself. Could he tell by looking at me?

After scrutinizing me for a moment, he remarked: "There's something humorous in your right eye."

"My *right* eye?" I cried. "What about my left?"

"That one's more serious," he assured me.

Patience and a Monument

It's a buyer's market, the supply of poetry far exceeding the demand. That is why the buyer can take his own sweet time in buying or not buying.

He may be a poet himself and know what it is to be made to wait. Yet in keeping his fellow poets waiting he is probably not being mean. He is not even necessarily being inconsiderate. If he is the editor of a quarterly, it may be convenient for him to let poems accumulate for a couple of months and then make his selection from a full net of fishes.

There is something curiously ambivalent about waiting a long time to hear from an editor. Pessimism says: If he really liked the poems, surely he would have given some hint before now. Optimism says: Why would he hold on to them if he weren't interested?

Once I was kept waiting considerably more than one year. The poems had been sent in toward the end of a certain calendar year, kept all the next year, and returned early in the third calendar year. I was reminded of Ephraim Pratt who was born in the seventeenth century and died in the nineteenth, having spanned in its entirety the century we are pleased to call the Enlightenment.

His monument stands on a peaceful slope under pines in the cemetery of the small town of Shutesbury, Massachusetts.

> Erected by the Town of
> Shutesbury in memory of
> Ephraim Pratt
> Born in East Sudbury
> Nov. 1, 1686, Removed to

Shutesbury soon after its
first settlement where
he resided until he
Died May 22, 1804
In his 117 year.
He was remarkably cheerful
in his disposition and
temperate in his habits.
He swung a scythe 101 consecutive
years and mounted a
horse without assistance
at the age of 110.

Poetry and Power

I dreamed that Power and Poetry were walking down the street together. It was beautiful to see how they accommodated themselves to each other. Poetry, for example, walked a little faster than usual and Power slowed down his stride, and so they kept abreast.

I overheard Power tell Poetry that he too was powerful. I could see that Poetry tried not to look flattered and that Power tried not to sound patronizing.

Poetry seemed to hear everything that Power was saying. Communication the other way was not quite so successful, Poetry having a low-pitched voice.

I saw Power reach out a hand as if to lay it on Poetry's shoulder or possibly to pat his head. But the hand couldn't reach head or shoulder. The hand could have reached only if Power had stooped.

They were friends all right, and it was beautiful to see how they kept abreast. They would have gone arm in arm, no doubt, had that been possible.

Logic

If one man's poem is another man's poison, then one man's book of poems is another man's apothecary shop of poisons.

On the other hand, if one man's poison is another man's poem, then one man's apothecary shop of poisons is another man's soda fountain.

John Quincy Adams

We do not think of John Quincy Adams as a poet, yet a volume of his poems was published in 1848, the year of his death. One, "To Sally," is a translation, partly strict and partly freewheeling, of Horace's familiar ode, "Integer Vitae." By doubling the length of each stanza Adams is able to extend Horace's geography magnificently.

> What though he plough the billowy deep
>   By lunar light, or solar,
> Meet the resistless Simoon's sweep
>   Or iceberg circumpolar!
> In bog or quagmire deep and dank
>   His feet shall never settle;
> He mounts the summit of Mount Blanc
>   Or Popocatapetl.

If you remember that early photograph of the old Adams in which he sits staring at us like the incarnation of gloom, or remember the incident told by his grandson Henry of how once the ex-President emerged from his study to grasp the hand of the reluctant boy and lead him every step of the way to school, never once releasing his grip and never once speaking, or remember how in his later years J. Q. rose regularly at five in winter and after starting his chamber fire from flint, began the day with a chapter from his Greek Testament—you are surprised not that he wrote poetry but that he could write it with a light touch. The Horation irony, the mock-seriousness, he catches to a T. Yet I suspect that the seriousness, both with him and with Horace, was not entirely mock. The wolf that ran away may have been all spoofing, but Sally (Lalage) was a lovely girl and no kidding.

"To Sally" may be found in Edmund Clarence Stedman's *An American Anthology,* a monumental work in 878 pages that appeared in 1900. The 590 American nineteenth-century poets included are arranged in eight sections: Early Years of the Nation, First Lyrical Period, Division I, Division II, Division III, Second Lyrical Period, Division I, Division II, Division III, and Close of the Century. John Quincy Adams occurs in Early Years of the Nation, of course. In a very brief biographical note, Stedman calls his verse "quaint and old-fashioned." Could 1848 have seemed as quaint to 1900 as 1900 seems to 1967?

Publisher as Wife

Poets beget poems but publishers give birth to books. Though some men prefer to get along without wives, I never heard of a poet who preferred to get along without a publisher. That many poets do get along without publishers must be attributed to their lack of luck in wooing.

Failing to win a publisher a poet has three choices. (1) He can buy a publisher. (2) He can publish himself. (3) He can remain unpublished.

Buying a publisher may be all right in realms where wives also are for sale. Here in America where wives are at least ostensibly not for sale the buying of a publisher smacks of prostitution.

Being one's own publisher can have the virtue of complete candor. "Published by the author." A poet simply hires a printer. It will do in a pinch, but the pinch should not last too long.

Publishers differ from one another as much as do wives. Some are better housekeepers than others. Some are more affectionate than others. And some do more than others to insure a lasting union. Sometimes a poet and a publisher remain wedded for life. In the lives of other poets there is much divorce—a situation not always necessarily unhappy.

Style

"C— R— was the reader for the members' lyric contest poems, looking most stylish in a charming lavender hat and dress."

Let no one look down his nose at this little news item. Surely it was worth noting that the reader looked stylish and that her lavender hat and dress were charming. If her hat and dress were more notable than her style of reading the members' lyric contest poems (to say nothing of the style of the lyric contest poems themselves) it was both honest and sensible to say so.

In her lavender hat and dress what was she but a lyric poem herself?

Poetry as a Competitive Pursuit

It is inevitable, I suppose, that like all other pursuits poetry should be competitive. Inevitable and not altogether unfortunate. Even the angels, it has been intimated, compete with one another for position in the hierarchies and for first prize in holiness.

But is there any virtue in making poetry as competitive as possible? Does poetry flourish necessarily in direct ratio to the number of prizes offered? May not the subtle competition for the esteem of the individual reader be sometimes better than a public competition for lucre?

In a certain Eastern college each April six or seven college students, representing as many colleges, gather to present their own poems to a sympathetic audience. Three judges determine the winner. The winner receives one hundred dollars, the runner-up twenty-five dollars, and the others nothing. I have often thought how pleasant it would be if no overt judging took place, and if each of the young poets received an honorarium of fifteen or twenty dollars.

The Well-made Poem

Spare me, please, the man who speaks, whether dispar-
agingly or approvingly, of the well-made poem. Has he
never read or heard that poems are not made but grow—
like snowflakes, like flowers, like seashells? Has he never
perceived that a true poem—like a rose, like a goddess,
like a diamond—is not made but born?

Crowds

Recently the editor of *Epoch,* with the long summer ahead of him, offered his readers a list of the fifty best living American poets. But being a generous man, he did not stop at fifty. His list contained four hundred and thirty-four names.

They were arranged in alphabetical groups. The *S* poets alone numbered fifty-three. There was only one *Z* poet. For *Q* and *Y* there were no poets at all.

The idea seemed to be that from the editor's four hundred and thirty-four the reader could pick his own final fifty.

"I suppose," said a friend of mine, "that a poet might endure being left out of a list of fifty, but to be omitted from a list of four hundred and thirty-four would be unendurable."

"Quite the contrary," I retorted, "if the poet is anything like me. I should feel insulted to be left out of a list of fifty; but if I were omitted from the four hundred and thirty-four, my response would probably be 'Thank God!'"

"Why so?"

"My distaste for crowds."

Modest Check

The editor sends me his modest check. The phrase is his own. I myself would scarcely have thought of that adjective.

Along with the modest check he writes me a very nice letter. He is clearly a very nice man, check or no check, modest or otherwise. A modest man, I'm sure.

But though modesty is a virtue in human beings, is it necessarily a virtue in checks?

As a check grows larger and larger does it become less and less modest? Does a check too large to be called modest become immodest?

And if there are upper limits to modesty, are there lower limits as well? Just how small may a modest check be and still be modest, rather than measly?

Another question. Why do poets deserve so much modesty?

Group Reviews

They are like mass executions, these group reviews of poetry when there are ten or twelve books in the group. A man can be shot to death with some dignity if he dies alone. To kill ten or twelve in a batch is like swatting flies.

If mass execution be too grim a metaphor, then say a group review is like a group photograph. Good features are lost sight of and weak features thrown into relief. A large head by itself might be impressive but not when surrounded by small heads, or a long nose by short noses.

A book is at a double disadvantage. Good things said about the other books will put it in the shade. Bad things said about the other books easily produce guilt by association.

In a mass review of poetry each poet can be compared to every other poet in the group to the general disadvantage of everybody. Even praise from a group reviewer may be something to fear. "Though X never rises above a certain level of mediocrity, it may be said in his favor that he never falls quite as low as Y."

Yarrow

Having just read three poems by Wordsworth—"Yarrow Unvisited," "Yarrow Visited," and "Yarrow Revisited"— I am ready to concede the poet a man both logical and thorough. The three titles are as inevitable as beginning, middle, and end; as comprehensive and comforting as faith, hope, and charity.

I think I know now what people mean when they say a writer has exhausted his subject.

Of course, Wordsworth could have written a fourth poem: "Yarrow Re-revisited." But he didn't. He knew when to stop.

Weighed in the Balance

"I didn't feel settled quite firmly enough on a choice among these poems," writes the editor of *Poetry*.

An appropriate statement, surely. Honest. Also tactful. I have no complaint.

I am entirely reconciled. Indeed, I am more reconciled than an editor might suppose possible. If there is the least doubt in the editorial mind of the worthiness or suitability of my poem, I much prefer he send it back. I don't want to squeak by. I don't want to creep into the fold.

Perhaps it is pride, but I prefer not to have a poem accepted for any other reason than love. Having known love, now and then, I cannot be content with anything less. Now and again an editor has loved a poem of mine before it was in print, and a reader has loved it afterward. On such love, on the memory of it, I can live for a while. I can keep going.

Perhaps it is pride, perhaps it is conceit, but I can't keep out of mind the possibility that the poem the editor rejects may have turned the tables on him. While he was judging the poem, the poem may have quietly been judging him. In the eyes of eternity it may be the editor and not the little poem that was weighed in the balance and found wanting.

A Small Door

I would be a translator too, like all the most approved poets, if I could find the right language to translate from. Certainly not French, since everybody already can read the originals. And not Russian, since everybody soon will be able to read the originals. I want a language so remote geographically, linguistically, and spiritually, that not a single poem has ever found its way into English, and might never do so except for my good offices. I want to be a small door connecting two vast but heretofore mutually exclusive worlds.

Other Arts, Other Artists

"Did you ever try to imagine what it would be like to be a painter?" a poet friend asked me the other day.

"Can't say I ever did," I said.

"Painters fascinate me," he went on. "The way they work. The way they keep busy. A painter sets up his easel and sits down and goes to work painting. You never catch him staring at his canvas, biting his nails."

"Remarkable," I said.

"If a painter is not busy painting, it's because he's busy doing something else, not because he can't paint. You see what I'm getting at?"

"Maybe," I said.

"Something keeps guiding him, keeps telling him what to do next, stroke by stroke. If he's objective, it's something outside himself. If he's abstract, it's something inside himself. But something, something keeps feeding him you might say. And that's not true of us poets by a long shot—much of the time, at least. We have to wait, and sometimes we have to wait a hell of a time."

"For inspiration?" I asked.

"Call it that if you want," he said. "I'd call it simply a flow of good ideas, and the excitement that comes from it and that starts other ideas."

"And the burst of confidence," I added.

"What I want to know," he said, "is whether there has to be this difference, or whether we poets have just got into the habit of thinking there is."

"You mean we pamper ourselves?"

"Not so much pamper as make things hard for ourselves. I wonder if we do. I wonder if we don't."

"You're asking why a poet can't sit down to his typewriter and turn out poems with something like the steadiness with which a painter turns out paintings?"

"Yes, damn it."

"Well, that seems to me just about what some poets are doing."

"I'm not talking about drivel, I'm talking about poetry," he said.

"I'm talking about poetry too. I could name more than one distinguished poet and several not so distinguished who give me the impression they can write a poem almost any time they feel like it. They've learned how to take it easy. They don't try to be brilliant. They just take something nearby or something that happens to come into their mind and set it down with a few little imaginative quirks or touches. I mean they take half a dozen little items and set them down side by side. And somehow it makes a poem. It gives a mood."

"Does that sort of poetry satisfy you?" he asked.

"Not exactly," I said, "but I don't dislike it as much as I do some other kinds."

"Sort of painting with words?"

"I suppose so."

"And here's another thing," he went on. "Painters don't seem to mind being watched at work. They may even like it, find it stimulating. But just imagine you or me working on a poem with somebody hanging over our shoulder. A painter, I tell you, has something to go on so definite that he can keep going even with distractions."

"Painters must have their troubles too," I mused. "For instance, if a painter finds his painting is seriously wrong, there may be nothing to do but scrap it and start all over again. Especially a water color. You or I, now, if we find a poem is not right, we just slip a fresh sheet in the typewriter and write a new version. But take a sculptor now, or a composer. Those are the boys that make me ask questions."

"How so?"

"The way they work on assignment, on commission, turn out work to order. Somebody wants figures for a big fountain, dimensions such and such. Or 'Compose us music for symphony orchestra that will take ten to twelve minutes to play.' Could *you* write a poem to order?"

"God, no! Could you?"

"I don't think I'd want to have to. But maybe we ought to be able and willing and delighted. Maybe we've got into the habit of thinking a poem is not a real poem, not pure, unless it drops out of a clear blue sky. Maybe we're prejudiced."

"Maybe we are," he said. "But I'd say that if we're prejudiced, it's a good prejudice."

"You're going to keep on turning down lucrative commissions?"

"Absolutely."

"And go on staring at a blank sheet of paper in your typewriter and biting your nails?"

"Absolutely."

Peacock

"The successful warrior becomes a chief; the successful chief becomes a king; his next want is an organ to disseminate the fame of his achievements and the extent of his possessions; and this organ he finds in a bard, who is always ready to celebrate the strength of his arm, being first duly inspired by that of his liquor. This is the origin of poetry...."

So wrote Thomas Love Peacock as long ago as 1820. A satirical rogue, no less.

It was Peacock's essay, "The Four Ages of Poetry," that spurred Shelley to his famed "Defense." But Shelley couldn't touch the rogue, not really.

Too bad Peacock grew shrill and abusive toward the end of his essay. Bards of the Iron Age he could handle with a nice irony. But not his contemporaries, no, not his contemporaries.

Thomas Love Peacock. Or, if you will, plain Tom Peacock.

In a Brazen World

How often one man is praised in terms of another man's disparagement. You honor Keats by damning Shelley; the more you damn the one the more you honor the other.

But here is something that goes beyond that. Here, on a dust jacket, is a poet praised in terms not of another poet's disparagement, but of all other poets. Only one poet living, we are informed, can hold a candle to this poet.

> How far that little candle throws his beams!
> So shines a shrill note in a brazen world.

Slender

"The individual essays in *The Satirical Rogue* are charming indeed, but taken together they make a very slender book, I am afraid," wrote the senior editor.

The senior editor was commenting on the essays that you are at this moment reading, dear reader.

Very well. But why should every book be fat? A slender woman is not usually thought to labor under a disadvantage.

Very well. Very well, indeed. But when were rubies and diamonds sold by the peck?

Introducing the Poet

Theophilus T, my poet-friend, was telling me the other day of various experiences he has had in being introduced to audiences, and of certain strategies he has devised for self-defense.

You see, just at the moment when he wants to be nothing but an inconspicuous vehicle or medium for his poetry, he may find his cap waving with plumes and his pockets bulging with plums.

To remove gracefully as many of the plumes and plums as possible (smiling at himself as he does so and never, of course, at his introducer) has become an art in itself.

Yet having acquired something of a technique, he begins to doubt this whole approach, and for three reasons. (1) No matter how deftly he tries to deornament himself and cut himself down to size, he must talk about himself to do so and thus make matters worse. (2) Audiences are so accustomed, he says, to the grand buildup that they take it for granted. He suspects his embarrassment is confined to himself. (3) Audiences may actually like panegyric: the more glory is poured on the head of the poet standing before them, the more reflected glory there will be for everybody to bask in.

Theophilus says he has just about made up his mind that at his next poetry reading he will accept unprotestingly anything and everything the introducer may offer, letting it flow over and off him like rain on the roof or wind through the trees. It will be a peaceful experience, he thinks.

II

What a Witch Told Me

At times I could believe that it didn't happen at all, that I was the dupe of a singularly vivid daydream, a walking dream induced by the drugged October weather. But I have only to pick up a certain small stone lying on my desk and turn it in my hand to know that I was not dreaming.

It was one of those retrospective days when thoughts turn back to summer and farther than summer as naturally as birds drift south. Warmth like a faint-blue blanket lies over the land. Colors that yesterday flashed now smoke and smolder. And the few leaves that fall fall of their own free will, for there is no wind to hurry them.

Drifting myself, I had reached an unfamiliar road that seemed without destination, too narrow and remote to invite even a casual traffic. Perhaps it went somewhere a back way. Perhaps it went nowhere.

Hearing a rustle in the bushes, I looked to see a chipmunk or squirrel or chewink scratching in leaves like a hen, and was startled at the color of clothing. Someone was picking something within the thicket. Then she stepped out part way and I saw her.

She was not over four feet high, and though a little warped with age and much weathered, she looked as hale as a pumpkin. Her face was the color of a ripe acorn and as plump. As for clothing, her skirt, blouse, apron, and jacket managed among them to display goldenrod-yellow,

This tall tale was written by the instructor, Robert Francis, for the poetry division of the Chautauqua Writers' Workshop, 1956, and published by its members.

red maple, bottle-gentian-blue, oriole, and the red-purple of wild grape jell. On one arm she carried a basket.

"Hello, Mr. Poet," she called in a small chuckling voice. As she spoke, I noticed that one eye drooped while the other looked up, as if to enable her to see the ground and the sky at the same time. The upward- and outward-looking eye was black and sharp as a bird's.

"Why do you call me that?" I asked.

"Because that's what you are."

"Who told you?" I demanded.

"Nobody told me, Mr. Poet. It's printed all over you." By tilting back her head she was able to focus both eyes on me at once, a little disconcertingly. "Only poets and painters go poking about this kind of place this time of day. But painters strap their paints and brushes to them like papooses. Oh, I know you, you, you. Why—I could tell you what you're thinking this moment, if I'd a mind to."

"You could, could you?" I cried. "Well, I'm going to tell you what you, you, you are. You're a wise woman. That's what *you* are."

A soft laugh seemed to bubble through her like yeast. "Other people have called me other things. They've called me—shhhhh!—a witch. But it's all right to be a witch today. They don't duck us any more or drown us, or flatten us with paper weights or brand us with flat irons, or dangle us on clothes lines from clothes poles. Oh, it's very nice to be a witch nowadays. The Constitution protects us."

Suddenly she tilted her basket toward me. "Look." Vermilion rose hips, hawthorn haws, deep-coral-pink barberries in clusters, the old-fashioned kind from petered-out gardens, crimson wild cranberries from bogs, and darker crimson cones of sumac, both the smooth and the hairy, besides other filchings and fancies I couldn't name, composed her hoard.

"What do you do with them?" I asked.

Brushing her hand over the booty as fondly as a rajah fingering his rubies, "Oh—chutneys, jellies, marmalades, and brews." She put a rose hip to her mouth and began to nibble the rind, letting the seeds fall. "The wilder the fruit the tarter the tang, the smaller the berry the sweeter the smell. Want me to tell you a secret, Mr. Poet? A secret about poetry?"

My amazement must have been obvious.

"What does a witch know about poetry, heh?" she taunted. "But if I know charms and spells and mushrooms and moon phases and gems and fortunes and waterwitching, why shouldn't I know poetry?"

"Tell me."

She finished nibbling the rose hip before speaking. "How much do you want it, Mr. Poet? Would you grovel in the dust to hear? Would you get down and glide like a serpent?"

Just then a chickadee bounced into the air, then back to its twig. Deliberately she picked a single crimson seed from a sumac cone and held it out on her palm. "Sweet? Sweet? Suet suet suet," she wheedled. "Piccalilli piccalilli piccalilli peppery peppery purr."

"Chickadee dee dee," answered the bird as it darted down to her hand and off with the tidbit.

She picked another seed and put it between her lips. So still she stood, so stolid, she might have been a wooden doll whittled by an old man in the mountains on a winter night and dressed by his wizened wife in gingham samples and snippets of calico.

With a feathery flurry the bird lit on her shoulder and peered shrewdly into her face. Three times it tried to snatch the seed by craning its neck and fanning its wings. Finally, it rose, hovering, and seized the prize from her lips—all without making her bat an eyelash or quiver an eyelid.

After the bird had gone, she remained frozen, until I feared she had become locked in an epilepsy or, having entranced herself, was unable to break her own spell.

Very slowly she relaxed into a quincelike smile, eying me as if to say, "See? The birds know."

"Tell me the secret," I insisted.

"The birds come because I become a bird," she riddled.

"I mean the secret about poetry."

Lifting her head to bring both eyes on me at once, she scrutinized me so sharply that I had an uncanny feeling she was looking clear through me at something beyond. "Those that believe me I make pay in beaten gold or green bills, or if they're poor, I make glide like serpents. Those that mistrust me I tell free or save my breath to cool my porridge. You I'll tell free."

Fastened and fascinated by those eyes, I felt myself believing that I would not believe, believing her prophecy of my unbelief.

"The secret's all in one word, same for poetry as for jam or jell. And the word, Mr. Poet, is flavor. Everything's flavor and without flavor's nothing. Strong flavor, strange flavor, wild flavor, flavor like nobody else's, flavor—"

Suddenly she broke off as if to check my reception. Since I wanted her to go on and most decidedly did not want to glide like a serpent, I tried to feel negative and unbelieving. But I was coming to a point where I didn't know what I thought.

"How—how do you find the right flavor?" I stammered.

"Some have it natural," she chirped, "some have to bewitch themselves for it, some go so far's to sell their souls to big Satan or little satan, but most never find it 'tall. Flavor's mostly in mixing. You mix two wilds or a wild with a tame. You mix sense with nonsense. More flavor's in pure nonsense than in sense, but most is in mixing. For instance, in spells and curses, I mix a mite of red Indian and gypsy—"

Again she broke off as if to pry deeper into my mind. A surge of resentment swept over me that she should be looking through me, or thinking she was looking through me, like glass. I felt her mind around me like a sticky spiderweb, and I resolved to assert myself and break loose.

"Old woman, old woman, old woman," I cried, shaking my finger at her, "don't tell me nonsense is better than sense. Nonsense is a phoney. And as for flavor, there's something greater in poetry than flavor. And that's form. I mean having everything related to everything else."

"Ho, ho," she taunted, "you like your poems pretty and tidy, don't you?"

"It's not pretty and tidy I'm talking about," I shouted. "It's having everything woven together like a living leaf or green tree. It's a little like the mixing you're talking about, confound you."

She stood an epitome of scorn. "Then why call it something it ain't, Mr. Poet? Oh, I know the young girls with their pretty long arms and their tidy long legs. That's form for you. Me—I'm no shape at all, but I've more flavor than fifty sirens."

A revulsion, now, at my silly anger came over me. Yet I was determined to keep the initiative. "Where do you live?" I shot at her.

She eyed me suspiciously a long moment before answering. "I'm the old woman lives under the hill."

"And if she's not gone she lives there still," I quoted.

> "Baked apples she sold and cranberry pies
> And she's the old woman who never told lies."

Then, out of pure impudence, I mocked the last line:

> "And she's the old woman who never told lies?
> And she's the old woman who NEVER told lies."

It was as if a cloud had come over her. She held up both hands in front of her face and peered through the spread fingers.

"Kind Sir," she cajoled in a squeezed voice, "will you do a poor old woman a favor? See that little stone in the road? The dimber one with streaks of roseblood? Pick it up like a kind sir and give it to me?"

I hesitated, then walked over to the stone. Except for its dull pink color, there was nothing remarkable about it that I could detect. I picked it up and turned it over in my hand. Why not toss it to her and so avoid getting any closer than I had been before? I glanced over at her.

But she was not there. She was not anywhere in sight. She had disappeared.

Whether she had stepped into a hollow tree or slipped down a woodchuck hole or merely moved deeper into the foliage, I had no way of knowing. To try to follow her might have been, to say the least, unhealthy.

I was breathless and had to rest several minutes before starting home. I brought the stone with me and put it on my desk. It is rose quartz, I think, with a mixture of other minerals.

You might say it haunts me, I look at it so much. If I hide it in a drawer, I still think about it and sooner or later bring it out again. In my writing I have been feeling strange new impulses which I somehow associate with the stone. Should I throw it away? Should I drop it down a deep well?

No question in my mind that the stone was a ruse of the old girl to get away unseen. But what endlessly teases me is whether she chose a chance stone for the purpose or a special one.

III

Francis on the Spot

An Interview

With Philip Tetreault and Kathy Sewalk-Karcher

1975-76, Amherst, Massachusetts

In The Trouble With Francis *you delineate two economic and philosophic principles: to make full use of everything possessed and to get rid of everything you don't need. Such simplicity and conservation is often aligned with oriental life. Does any of your philosophy stem particularly from Eastern thought or practice?*

These two principles were developed in response to my actual situation. Since I was very poor, I wanted to enjoy to the utmost the free wealth that surrounded me; things that were mine for the picking, such as wild food, or fallen branches for fuel. Also the inexhaustible entertainment of all that was going on around me in nature and human nature.

A lesser way of adding to a poor man's assets was to save such things as cardboard boxes, paper bags, string, glass containers, etc. But though this thrift had a useful purpose, it brought a problem. My storage space would in time become overcrowded unless I began getting rid of the least useful things I was saving. But the saving was always easier than the throwing away.

My mother inspired my economy far more than did any Eastern philosophy. She made her own dresses and then remade them, the old dress becoming a new one. At a time when women wore hats, Mother redecorated her hats endlessly. When other women appeared in new bonnets at Easter, she would be wearing an old one that was at the same time a new one. And in her meal getting nothing was thrown away, leftovers being saved to enrich some future and no less savory dish.

In all this I was doing with my life what my poems were doing as they came into being. A poem in its early stages has a healthy appetite and wants to take into itself every available resource. At the same time it wants to eliminate whatever does not really belong to it. Thus a poem develops and achieves true selfhood.

In places, especially when you describe expenses and the serenity of Fort Juniper, your autobiography reminds me of Thoreau's Walden. *You seem to admire Thoreau, Emerson, Whitman, Frost, and others. Do you feel their doctrines helped you to establish your lifestyle?*

I do admire Emerson, Thoreau, Whitman, and Frost but I never tried to pattern my life on theirs. The way I live was reached step by step, stage by stage, as I strove to meet my needs with available resources and opportunities.

   a) When I moved to Amherst in 1926 I gained a rural environment.
   b) When I gave up school teaching in 1927, I gained leisure, that is, freedom to use my time for what was to me most important.
   c) In 1932 by leaving my father's household in South Amherst and becoming a "helper" in the homes of a series of old women, I gained a very humble financial independence.
   d) I gained other kinds of independence when I rented the "old house by the brook" in 1937.
   e) With the building of Fort Juniper in 1940 I had at last a completely congenial setting for my life: nature, leisure, privacy, and independence of every sort.

You have mentioned in TWF (The Trouble with Francis) *that you often felt more comfortable among plain people than you did in a college community and found plain people more stimulating to your imagination. Why?*

Among college people I felt inferior because they were above me in knowledge, achievement, and social status.

Plain country folk I found not only more comfortable to be with but more stimulating to my imagination because they never tried to be or appear other than they were. Their personalities were vivid. Everything they did and said was so expressive it made me want to put them into my poems. Take for instance old George Dwight of South Amherst who is the subject of at least three of my poems.

Artist

He cuts each log in lengths exact
As truly as truth cuts a fact.

When he has sawed an honest pile
Of wood, he stops and chops awhile.

Each section is twice split in two
As truly as a fact is true.

Then having split all to be split,
He sets to work at stacking it.

No comb constructed by a bee
Is more a work of symmetry

Than is this woodstack whose strict grace
Is having each piece in its place.

Beyond the changes that have taken place throughout the country, what changes have taken place in Amherst?

It is the expansion of the University of Massachusetts that is chiefly responsible for Amherst's becoming a dramatically different town from what it was when I moved here in 1926. Then the small Agricultural College, the "Aggie," was a sort of apologetic country cousin to Amherst College.

Today the University is a city with skyscrapers inside an otherwise still largely rural town surrounded by woodland and green fields. On almost any afternoon of the school year the city overflows into the town, and its sidewalks are taken over by thousands of students. And no wonder for there are now innumerable little boutiques aimed at the student trade. One notices especially the foreign graduate students: Far Easterners, here and there a sari from India, and of course the blacks, both native and imported, with their imposing globular hairdos like enormous black dandelions gone to seed.

Market Hill Road, three and a half miles from Amherst Center but still in the township of Amherst, was a dirt road when Fort Juniper was built in 1940. Now it is Macadam and its small farmers, janitors, and factory workers are outnumbered by university faculty. It has also become a throughway for new "developments" farther out in Amherst or in Shutesbury.

In spite of changes to the road, Fort Juniper maintains much the same character it had when built. Indeed, in contrast to its surroundings, it has been reverting to more primitive times since I have encouraged trees and bushes to come as they will and flourish. They now pretty much hide the road to the eye. Would that they could hide it to the ear!

While visiting you at Cowles Lane I couldn't help but notice your affinity to all that surrounded you. The birds that visited on the ledge outside your window were your friends. Even the pigeons in a nearby belfry were appreciated by you. What have you learned from nature that you have incorporated into your daily life?

Nature is a large part of that free wealth I spoke of in answering your first question. The more one watches and listens the more one finds to watch and listen to. The enjoyment of my natural surroundings, along with my writing, my music, and my friends, was so rich that I never craved any external entertainment.

I've talked with you briefly about religion and yet I have difficulty perceiving whether you feel God has been a part of your life or not. Do you consider yourself a "qualified" atheist? Your father was a Baptist minister, yet I begin to wonder whether religion has influenced your life.

It would be ungracious of me to say that I think your questions are answered in the last chapter of my autobiography. They are also answered in the book I am now working on: *The Trouble With God.*

All my life religion has been a central concern to me. As an extremely conscientious boy I accepted the religion taught and preached by my father, was baptized by him, became a member of the church, prayed and read the Bible daily, attended innumerable religious services, was active in the Christian Endeavor Society, and for a time taught a Sunday-school class of small boys.

Part way through high school I began to have what I called my "doubts." Yet at Harvard College I found the liberal religion preached at chapel (which was no longer compulsory) acceptable. And when, following college, I taught for a year at the American University of Beirut in Lebanon, I found their liberal nonproselytizing outlook something that I could embrace.

Just when it was that I began to disbelieve, not merely the evangelical Christianity I had been brought up in, but the Christian myth itself, it is impossible to say, my development having been so gradual and inevitable. Nor can I say just how long ago it was that I reached my present *weltanschauung.*

I regard myself as a religious man for three reasons:

a) If religion is essentially one's total attitude toward life, then I have such a total attitude.

b) I share and try to follow the same ethical ideals as does the avowed Christian, without accepting the supernatural substructure that is supposed to be necessary to support them.

c) Though I disagree fundamentally with the religious views of most other people, I am endlessly interested in what they believe.

I have a particular curiosity about your lack of stacks and stacks of books which most men of letters manage to accumulate over the years.

I have been too poor to buy many books and sometimes too poor to buy any, but poverty is not the principal reason for the smallness of my library. Since there are thousands upon thousands of books, new and old, that I can borrow from Amherst's outstanding public library and from the Frost Library of Amherst College, why should I buy, especially since so many books give me in only small measure what I am looking for? I dip into or skim through far more books than I read from beginning to end. My small small house (like a short short story) does not have room for a conventional library; and since I have no family to leave my books to, I lack one motive for accumulating them.

Yet small as my collection is, it is larger than one might suppose in entering my house. Books are stowed away in my bedroom and others are in boxes in the attic. I am more interested in reducing my store than in enlarging it. Whenever I have a book that a friend would enjoy owning, I prefer to give it to him now rather than wait till I die.

The recently established Robert Francis Collection at the University of Massachusetts Library in Amherst consists both of "papers" of many categories and of books in three groups: (1) a complete set of the books of which I am author, (2) fifty to sixty books inscribed to me, and (3) over a hundred and thirty anthologies and school or college texts in which my poems and essays are reprinted. For me it is a great satisfaction that these books are being kept safely and in proper order so that they can be available to interested scholars; and that at the same time they should no longer be crowding my small small house.

Throughout the autobiography you repeat that it was an extreme pleasure for you to "wander unseen" or to leave your "house and return to it unseen, the secrecy of movement itself a luxury." Why is the ritual of secrecy so necessary to your life-style? Is the magic of secrecy essential to your creative process?

I had a craving for and a deep enjoyment of solitude, both indoors and out. And so I took many walks by myself. If no one saw me go or come, then my aloneness was all the more complete. Though I also enjoyed walking with friends, there was a quality to a solitary walk that I could have in no other way. It was only in being alone that I could fully live with my thoughts and out of that living create poems. The world of nature, when I was alone in it, made me feel perfectly at home. People— not my friends, but people in general—might interrupt my thought, misunderstand me, make me feel inferior, or even impose their wills on me; but nature was always sympathetic, nonintrusive, and gently stimulating. As I have gained self-confidence over the years and no longer fear people or feel inferior to them, they, like nature, have become an endlessly rich and stimulating experience. Still I love to be alone.

From your solitude, Robert, you have the vantage point of being able to extract yourself from the main maelstrom and find another perspective on the literary world. What are some of the trends you have witnessed in the literary world throughout the fifty years you have been writing?

When I looked out from my solitude it was not the literary world that I looked at. The literary world was something I felt I did not belong in, and it did not greatly interest me.

What did greatly interest me and what I thought about constantly and always had at least in the back of my mind was the need to see clearly and comprehensively and to size up philosophically and ethically the totality of things, the universe, and man's situation in it. The last chapter of my autobiography gives some idea of this.

It is only fairly recently that I have had a craving to see clearly and size up the contemporary literary world, especially the world of poetry. But to capture it in a concept or series of concepts continues to elude me as the god Proteus slipped through the fingers of any would-be captor.

Knowing Robert Frost seems to be a memorable part of your life. Did visiting with Frost show you what it was like to be a writer? I would imagine that Frost admired your lifestyle. Did you ever envy Frost because of the life he lived and the success that was bestowed upon him?

Frost was too special, too exceptional, to stand as a representative writer. Rather, his qualities distinguished him from most other writers. Unlike the stock poet Frost was tough, more realistic, seemingly a match for any man, and usually more than a match. He and I were too far apart in achievement and status for me to have had any feeling of envy. It was enough to feel the tonic of his power.

In 1938 Robert Frost sent you a letter in admiration of your new book, Valhalla and Other Poems. *In this letter he said, "You are achieving what you live for." What would you suspect Frost meant by this?*

There is no mystery about this. To Frost the greatest thing in life was to bring something into form. Out of the welter of daily living, out of the big buzzing world, to get something clear, achieved, and final. He did it with words—his "momentary stay against confusion." He thought I had begun to do it with words too.

Chapter ten of your autobiography describes your trips to Italy and your attempts to make connection with your past in two journeys to Ireland. What does "meeting your roots" mean to you, Robert, and do you ever have a certain feeling that you are integrated with the consciousness of your past and family tradition?

I went to Ireland not with any sense of a mystical search but only from a natural curiosity to see what sort of place my great-grandfather, Matthew, had lived and worked in, and where my grandfather, Daniel, had spent his first twenty years. Any feeling of affinity with Ireland that I may have expressed is largely playful with me. But I have seriously speculated on possible personality traits I may have derived from Dr. Daniel Francis.

Are there any thematic or stylistic aspects in your writing which arise particularly from "meeting your roots"?

No. The only writing I did in Ireland or about Ireland was a set of six or eight vignettes in which I tried to capture vivid aspects of Irish life. What the tourist does with his camera I tried to do with words. But I did the same sort of thing in Italy.

You spent much of 1975 away from Fort Juniper. Was your stay at an apartment in Amherst Center a satisfying retreat from the Fort?

Better say that my return to Fort Juniper has been a satisfying retreat from the apartment and Amherst Center.

When I moved to Amherst Center in mid-December of 1974 I thought the arrangement would be more or less permanent. I would maintain two homes year round: the apartment for its obvious conveniences, and Fort Juniper chiefly for summer gardening, sunbathing, and music. But though the apartment had some unusual advantages, it proved to have some unforseen disadvantages. So before my lease expired at the end of August I had decided to move back to the Fort for good.

Being away for eight and a half months enabled me to see *its* great advantages more clearly. I needed to have moved out in order to move back; and moving back, like the return of a theme in music, has been more than a mere return.

So the apartment proved a valuable experiment. (1) I found out what living in Amherst Center today actually involves. And (2) I rediscovered my beloved home.

Please describe how you believe your poetry has developed since you first began writing.

My early poetry was quiet and brooding in a style that might be called relaxed traditional. As I grew older my poetry expressed a greater craving for warmth, color, and movement.

While continuing to write in a more or less traditional idiom, I have added two entirely new techniques: word-count and fragmented surface. My latest collection, *Like Ghosts of Eagles,* has more variety than any earlier book. However, a perceptive reader of my poetry might be able to give a more objective account of my development than I can.

Robert, your poetry is unique with respect to much contemporary poetry. How would you describe your poetry compared to that of your fellow poets?

Unique is a word I use with caution. In one sense every poet is necessarily unique just as every human being is unique. In another sense no poet is unique.

Let me list some of the basic positions or attitudes that underlie my poetry, and you can decide for yourself to what extent those positions and attitudes differ from contemporaries.

a) For me a poem is something made as well as something said, and from the making or forming comes much of the excitement for both poet and reader. I want the making and the saying not only to be of equal weight but, as far as possible, to enhance each other. For me poems that are only saying, only reportorial or confessional, would not be worth writing.

b) Though I am expressing myself in everything I write, my aim is to get outside myself by means of my poems. That is, I want to give birth to poems that will detach themselves from me and have a life of their own.

c) My poems confront the actual, recognizable world that we share with one another. However imaginative and original my vision and interpretation of that world, I do not want to lose connection with it. Surrealism strikes me as something appropriate for certain effects. But the reader should have a clue as to why the surrealism is being employed. Uncontrolled, hit-or-miss surrealism seems to me both irresponsible and pointless.

d) I am philosophically a pessimist and many of my poems present a tragic and even bleak picture of the human situation. Yet I think more of my poems celebrate those aspects and experiences of life that are admirable, beautiful, and life enhancing. Honesty compels me to write poems covering the entire spiritual spectrum; but the poems of celebration have an extra, you might say a functional, motive.

You have written in different genres and touched on many subjects in your writing. Have you been occupied with any particular subject or works lately?

I am writing some new poems to be included in my collected poems due in 1976. The volume will have eight sections and these new poems will constitute section eight. The other seven sections will correspond with my seven books of poetry already published. Though the sections will keep their chronological order, the poems within each section will have a new order. This reordering has caused me considerable work. I have also written a foreword or preface which, though very brief, came only after much trial and error.

Also, from time to time, I am adding to two continuing projects: (1) A second series of *Satirical Rogue* pieces. Five groups of these have already been published in magazines, and there are enough now or almost enough for a new volume. (2) A collection of portraits and sketches called *Observations and Visions of the Young Male*.

I hope to soon complete the manuscript of *The Trouble With God*.

This interview itself is something that has demanded considerable time and thought.

Do you write for an audience or for yourself?

I write for both, the two being inseparable. Only by aiming to make my poems intelligible and meaningful to at least a few readers can I make them fulfilling for myself. The challenge and excitement is precisely here.

I think of myself as giving birth to poems. They begin as parts of myself, but become detached from me to live lives of their own. Once written and published, they are for anyone who wishes to incorporate into his own life. I would not know how to write just for myself, and I have no desire to learn.

Since you did not major in English but in history, how did your Harvard years help you to become a poet?

Harvard College had no chance to help me directly to become a poet since it was not until several years after graduation that I had any notion of becoming one. Harvard did help me a little in learning to write, chiefly through Freshman English, the only writing course I took. During my year at the Harvard Graduate School of Education I think my writing ability improved. By that time I had a typewriter, and the effort to turn out neatly typed assignments probably encouraged me to improve their composition.

Of course Harvard contributed much to my general education, and perhaps that was a sounder and safer contribution toward my becoming a poet than any courses could have provided.

Poets have different opinions about revision and the creative act. Do you spend much time revising your poems, going through draft after draft?

With me writing and revising are one and inseparable. My poems are not first written and then revised; they are revised into existence. Therefore revise is not the best word. When the impulse for a poem comes, I jot down what I can on a sheet of paper. No sooner done than I have ideas for changing and developing those first words. So a second sheet goes into my typewriter, then a third, and so on. The process is a combination of addition, elimination, and ceaseless rearranging. I never know how long this will go on and how many sheets I'll need until the time comes when I can think of nothing further to do. Of course, by the next day or the next month I may have new ideas about the poem. But ultimately there comes a stop; the poem simply stops growing. Though far from perfect, it has somehow fulfilled itself.

It appears that your short poems far outnumber your longer ones such as your sestina and so forth. Do you prefer the former?

I like my poems to be of varying lengths. Just because so many of them are quite short I welcome the longer ones. But sometimes a poem that promises to be longer turns out short after all. Why? Its healthy power of elimination has got rid of more and more elements that didn't really belong to it, or that were at least not vital to it.

I have used your word-count poems in some of my classes to talk about the way poets vary line length. At first the word-count formula is not usually recognized. My students have asked, "Is it enough to have a correlation between the number of words per line and the number of lines in the poem?" What do you strive for when writing word-count poems?

Word-count is strict and mechanical. Whatever poetic value a word-count poem has must come from the way the poet achieves variety, freedom, and expressiveness within the rigid pattern. I find word-count congenial for static or satiric subjects.

Word-count means simply a fixed number of whole words, long or short per line. The fact that my first three word-count poems had the same number of lines in a stanza and the same number of stanzas in the poem as there were words in each line—this was partly a coincidence and partly an extension of the word-count idea, not an essential part of word-count itself.

As can be expected, writers sometimes go through periods in which they experience difficulty writing. Do you have any advice for beginning writers who experience such difficulty?

Working on several projects more or less at the same time can be helpful. It is also helpful to be working on a long poem, etc. Since the difficulty is often in getting started, something that has already been started may be relatively easy to continue.

Dry periods can be used for important reading, letter-writing, etc.

If dryness is persistent, you may do well to reexamine your whole approach to writing—your motives, methods, subject matter.

Clearly it must come as a shock to many who read your autobiography to hear that you dislike poetry and that contemporary poetry at its best bores you because it is not often at its best. When is poetry at its best, Robert? And how does a poet assure that a poem is at its best?

Poetry is at its best when it provides enjoyable excitement and when that excitement comes as much from what the poet makes of words as from what he says in words. Poetry at its best is a highly skilled game a poet plays with life and language, a game that the reader can follow play by play, able to distinguish the brilliant shots from the merely good ones, and the good ones from the poor ones, if any.

How have you conducted the writer's workshops that you have taught? What benefits can a writer expect from such an experience?

In the poetry classes that I used to conduct at writers conferences or workshops I aimed to make the group experience as active as possible. It seemed to me that the class session would be most fruitful if it emphasized lively discussion. So I thought of myself less as teacher (and certainly less as lecturer) than as orchestral conductor making it possible for all voices to be heard. No one ever raised a hand without getting instant recognition. And often when a question was addressed to me I turned it back to the group to answer.

Each day the basis of our study and discussion was a new mimeographed sheet of a couple of their own poems given without names. After a poem had been explored and criticized, its author was free to reveal himself or not. Almost always he chose to reveal himself. And this might lead to further probing and criticism.

Each of us also had for reference a mimeographed sheaf of poems I had chosen from various poets to serve as models and to illustrate various points.

Then there were the conferences. Every student was entitled to at least one, and I gave full measure, to say nothing of the time I spent in preparing for each. Whereas in class a student had criticism from the whole group, in conference he had only me. My approach was to pick out a student's best poem or some promising quality in his poetry, and to say in effect: "Let this poem or this quality be your guide to further growth." Doubtless I was too tactful and kind. Students remembered my encouragement and often forgot my criticism of their faults.

In all this I was of course the teacher even though I preferred to avoid the word. Frequently in class I would take five minutes or so to clarify some technical point with the help of the blackboard. I say "clarify." I was not laying down the law.

How helpful a poetry class at a summer conference can be depends on several factors: the attitude and ability of the "conductor," the attitude of the individual student, and the attitude of the group. Anyone open to change and growth will probably be benefited. But many in a poetry group are in love with their poems as they already are and do not want to make any significant change. They want the teacher to help them touch up a poem by changing a word here and there. But I refused to be a poetry nurse. I would as soon change diapers.

Do you believe that a writer should or should not feel an obligation to read his contemporaries in order to maintain an added perspective on his art?

I read or dip into contemporary poetry to keep in touch with what is going on. There is also the hope that I may find something both enjoyable to read and stimulating to my own work. Only when poetry is sent me by the author does any sense of obligation come into play.

You began two novels early in your career and in 1948 published We Fly Away, *a novel that captured some of your experiences as a handyman in an Amherst household. Why did you choose not to write any other novels? Did you feel more successful as a poet or is there something inherent in poetry that lent itself to your liking?*

It is my passion for economy with words and for using them to make something as well as to say something that explains why I have done so little in fiction. For fiction is inevitably verbose and like the "confessional" poem it is mainly a telling of something that has happened rather than a making of something new.

What phases have you gone through with respect to the publishing of your books? Will you share some experiences with us?

There have been two major phases, the first from 1936 to 1965, the second from 1965 to the present. During the first phase six books were published under good auspices, but with little sense of continuity from book to book and little indication that any publisher was interested in my future. Though Macmillan published my first three books (all of poetry), the third book almost didn't get published. I tell in my autobiography how after submitting the manuscript twice to Macmillan and having it both times rejected, it was finally accepted when presented by a literary agent.

Since publishing *The Orb Weaver* in 1960, Wesleyan has remained friendly and considerate, yet with scarcely a hint of substantial interest in my continuing work.

After knocking on various publishers' doors for thirty years, I had the unprecedented good fortune in 1965 of having a publisher knock on my door. Since then the University of Massachusetts Press has published five of my books, and will bring out my collected poems in 1976. The boost to my self-confidence as a writer has been incalculable, and it has come not only from the books published but just as importantly from the assurance that whatever I write will have an interested hearing at the Press. Though each book has had to run, and will have to run, the gauntlet of preacceptance readings and press committee decisions, I know that this press is as much interested in my future as in my past and that it is, in a sense, betting on me.

In TWF *you mention wanting "to strike a blow against war that would be felt," but in the remaining half of your statement you say, "but I was a writer and my tool and weapon was the written word." This seems to indicate a lack of confidence in the power of the pen.*

It was not in the power of the written word that I lacked confidence but only in the power of my own written words. Such antiwar poems as "Bloodstains," "Light Casualties," "The Righteous," and "The Articles of War" would be read by readers and listened to by audiences whenever I included them in readings; but would they have any appreciable weight in turning the tide against war? My readers and hearers were, and still are, relatively few.

Furthermore, though these are antiwar poems they are not antiwar propaganda. Propaganda aims to incite action; poetry leads to reflection. My antiwar poems are first of all poems. I wanted to write, in poetry or prose, something that would change people's attitudes and actions, but I did not succeed in doing it.

Since my written words, though strongly against war, could not be expected to lend appreciable weight to the antiwar movement, I felt the need all the more of doing something else. But what would that be?

What was the stance of your poetry and philosophy during the Vietnam war? Did you actively support the Writers Against the War?

I joined the War Resisters League before the beginning of the Second World War and signed the pledge which reads: "War is a crime against humanity. I therefore am determined not to support any kind of war international or civil, and to strive for the removal of all the causes of war."

From 1966 to 1973 I stood regularly with a group of Sunday vigilers on Amherst Common from noon to 1:00 P.M. to mourn and protest the war in Southeast Asia. But was that any more effective than my written words? If no one could prove how effective it was, no one could prove that it was not effective. It was a tiny trickle of protest that fed into the stream of other vigils and other types of protest, a stream that ultimately became a mighty river. For me it meant above all taking a public stand that would be seen by many people who had never read or would ever read my poems.

Of course it was not enough. I should have done more. I should have risked more. I should have made things harder for myself. I was never asked to join the Writers Against the Vietnam War, or to take part in one of their readings. Perhaps I should have taken the initiative and made contact with them. Yet once more the question: how effective would *that* have been?

What is the purpose of satire as you use it, Robert? Are there any genre or thematic restrictions or obligations that artists must consider before they delve into the satirical mode?

There are various kinds and tones of satire. Satire can strike out angrily at what is thought to be an evil, or satire can be simply a little gentle spoofing. "The Righteous" is a bitter, however quiet, satire against those godly church-going people who support any war our country is engaged in.

The Righteous

After the saturation bombing divine
worship after the fragmentation shells
the organ prelude the robed choir after
defoliation Easter morning the white
gloves the white lilies after the napalm
Father Son and Holy Ghost Amen.

By contrast "The Pope" is not against the Holy Father but rather an appreciation of him.

The Pope

The Pope in Rome
Under St. Peter's dome
Is the Pope at home.

Pomp is his daily fare
Poised in his papal chair
Quite debonaire.

The great bell pealing,
The cardinals kneeling,
The soaring ceiling—

All that display
Does not dismay
The Pope a single day.

My satires as they come to fulfillment tend to become more dignified, elegant, and subtle than they were at the start. Indeed, it might be argued that "Edith Sitwell Assumes the role of Luna" is not so much a satire of Dame Edith as a celebration of her vivid personality. I have recently written a poem about the doves that sit in contemplation in the open arches of the campanile of St. Brigid's Church. If the poem satirizes the church, it praises at the same time the doves.

Hearing you read at the Worcester County Poetry Festival and at Anna Maria College I couldn't help but think that you enjoy giving poetry readings. Was my assumption correct?

Yes.

Do you prepare for a reading in any particular way, for instance, by selecting particular poems and a particular order for them to be read in?

Each poetry reading I give is a fresh experience for me. The selection of poems is always new as is the order in which they are put together. I try to avoid any sense of a replay. Other poets often feature their new poems. I get my newness in other ways.

I want to draw from all my poems those that I think will be most effective for this occasion. Old poems have the advantage of having been tested again and again for their effectiveness with an audience. If I include a new poem or two I probably do not tell the audience they are new. I assume an audience wants enjoyable poems and is largely indifferent to their age.

How, then, can I bring any freshness to a reading of poems that may have been written and published years before? The answer is I say or read each poem as if I were doing it for the first time. Almost as if I were writing the poem on the spot. As if the experience in the poem were something I was having at the moment. To do this I must put out of mind all echoes of my former readings and concentrate exclusively on what the poem itself is saying.

Your prefaces seduce the audience into wanting to hear the poem and also provide many necessary details associated with a particular poem. Do you feel that you sometimes tease the audience with this approach? Do you use any other methods to gather the listener's attention or make your audience more appreciative of what you have read?

You speak of my "prefaces." If I am going to comment on a poem I may do so before the poem or after the poem, or at some time later in the program. I want to break up and enliven what so often in a poetry reading is a mere string of poems.

But better than commenting on a poem I like to say something that leads outward from the poem, or to take something outside the poem and bring it in. So I welcome unforeseen events that interrupt the poetry reading, such as the chiming of a clock or the arrival of late comers. I want life to keep breaking in.

For much the same reason I abandon the amplifier whenever feasible and stand, not behind a desk, but as close to the audience as possible. And, as you know, I throw out questions and challenges to the audience. Inviting them to try to memorize my tiny poem, "Museum Vase," by hearing me say it once or twice, arouses their most intense attention. People look at me as if they were looking clear through me. Very exciting.

Museum Vase
For W. A.

It contains nothing.
We ask it
To contain nothing.

Having transcended use
It is endlessly
Content to be.

Still it broods
On old burdens—
Wheat, oil, wine.

Asking the audience if you should go on reading is certainly within your character, Robert, and an admirable trait that others could benefit by. You also let the audience request poems to be read. Have you learned anything from their requests that helps you in your readings?

Actually I don't often ask an audience if I should go on reading. The reading has been timed to last a little under an hour. I want to give full measure but I also want to stop while my hearers are still a bit hungry. It is only when an audience keeps on and on with requests and questions that it seems only fair to reach some agreement with them as to when I should stop. Keeping on too long can have two unfortunate results: it can hold captive people who need or want to leave, and the reading can peter out.

Understand, it's not that I don't welcome requests. I welcome them very much for the following reasons.

   a) They tell me, obviously, which of my poems interest readers and listeners the most.
   b) They enrich the interplay between poet and audience.
   c) At a time when the poet's voice is necessarily so prominent, requests provide a pleasant vocal variety.

What should "happen" to both poet and audience when a poet gives a reading?

Giving a poetry reading for me is an act of fulfillment. First comes the writing of the poems. Then publication. Out of all my poems I now select a few for this audience, and I present them with an added dimension: my voice. Finally, I am communicating not with an unseen, scattered body of readers but with people vividly present before me, people whose response to me stimulates my performance and enriches my whole experience. For me a poetry reading is the climax of being a poet.

You remark how you were intrigued and engrossed with your mother's reading aloud to you in the days before radio and television. Do you attribute any of your later creative writing to this early fascination?

My mother's reading aloud, so enjoyable in my boyhood, did not contribute as much to my becoming a poet as did something else more fundamental in her personality. Her gift was to make things and to make them beautiful. My father's gift was to say things, for he was a preacher. As a poet I have the good fortune to unite the gifts of both parents.

The gentility and simplicity found in your poetry certainly is admirable and well appreciated by those that have read your books and heard you read. I've come away from hearing you read feeling that I have a model to follow and a message to mull over. You stimulate thought but your style is in direct contrast to, say, Robert Bly. His dynamism is so powerful it cracks the enamel off one's front teeth. Can you move mountains using your technique or is that beyond your expectations as a poet?

Can I move mountains? I never thought this was the aim of a poetry reading. And so I never tried. But if I were to try, I think I would use a steady, even pressure rather than detonation.

The Mountain

does not move the mountain is not moved
it rises yet in rising rests and there
are moments when its unimaginable weight
is weightless as a cloud it does not come
to me nor do I need to go to it I only
need that it should be should loom always
the mountain is and I am I and now a cloud
like a white butterfly above a flower.

IV

The Satirical Rogue Again

Two Words

Having heard time and again that "two words are not as good as one," I cannot refrain any longer from declaring this to be the precise opposite of the truth, at least as far as poetry is concerned. If poetry is the intensive interplay of words, then two words are the absolute minimum. One word cannot strike sparks from itself; it takes at least two for that. It takes two words lying side by side on the page to breed wonders.

Confetti Poet

After writing a poem, he would cut the paper into tiny pieces like confetti and, leaning out his window, let them flutter to the ground.

It was publication in a way, easier and so much more spontaneous than the usual procedure. It was also a challenge to the reader to put the poem together for himself, to make it really his own.

Yet to watch a poem drift down like pear or apple petals in May was charming in itself. A reader could now enjoy a poem without the bother of reading it.

One day a graduate student looking for something to do decided to take up the challenge. But putting the pieces together took a long time, since they were so bafflingly uniform in size and shape.

Imagine his disillusion and disgust when the first poem to be reconstructed showed no poem there. He denounced the Confetti Poet as a fake.

And what did the Confetti Poet say to that? He smiled. Where was a poem so delightful and so inexhaustible as a pure white sheet of paper?

Sedentary

It might be justly urged that many poets are today too sedentary, sitting all day long as they do, and sometimes far into the night, on their *ars poetica.*

Critic

If I were a critic my pleasure would be to enrich rather
than to explicate. The really difficult poem I would
gladly leave to my fellow critics to crack. I would take
something seemingly simple and easy and point out
subtleties no one else had ever noticed.

> There was an old woman went up in a basket
> Ninety times high as the moon,
> And where she was going I couldn't but ask her
> For in her hand she carried a broom.
>
> "Old woman, old woman, old woman," quoth I,
> "Whither, Oh whither, Oh whither so hight?"
> "To sweep the cobwebs off the sky."
> "Shall I go with you?" "Aye, by and by."

The child's first question takes two lines; the old
woman's first answer, one line; the child's second question, only five monosyllables; the old woman's final
answer, only four. The old woman, you see, is getting
farther and farther away.

The Cow

> The friendly cow all red and white,
>   I love with all my heart;
> She gives me cream with all her might,
>   To eat with apple-tart.
>
> She wanders lowing here and there,
>   And yet she cannot stray,
> All in the pleasant open air,
>   The pleasant light of day;

And blown by all the winds that pass
And wet with all the showers,
She walks among the meadow grass
And eats the meadow flowers.
[Robert Louis Stevenson]

If I were a critic I should like to point out that when a cow walks among meadow flowers and eats the meadow grass, that is prose; but when she walks among meadow grass and eats the meadow flowers, that is poetry.

Major

"Can you tell me," I asked, "precisely what a major poet is?"

"That's easy," he replied. "A major poet is any poet of major importance."

"What gives a major poet his major importance?" I pursued. "It is a question of quality only, or does quantity enter in?"

"It's mostly a matter of quality," he said.

"Then why do people speak of a very fine minor poet?"

"That would be a poet who wrote only very brief poems."

"Oh, so quantity does enter in," I exclaimed, "quantity as to the individual poems if not as to the poet's total output. I suppose a fine poet who wrote only brief poems would have to be very fine indeed to be a major poet."

He looked at me with just a trace of irritation.

"Now that you've made clear to me the difference between major and minor, I'd like to know where you draw the line between them. The line, say, between a grade-A poet who writes brief poems and a grade-B poet who writes long ones?"

He cleared his throat. "You're making things too complicated."

"But I thought things were complicated to start with!" I cried.

Poetry as Work

Since we Americans make work of everything we do, not least our sports and recreations, it is not surprising that we have got around to making work of poetry. To write poetry nowadays is work and to read it is also work, often hard work. Because poetry is work it is thought worthy of being taught in colleges and universities, both the writing of it and the reading of it, which is called "close reading." Though the writing of poetry is often unremunerative work, the teaching of the writing of it or of the reading of it is not.

After a course or two in the writing of poetry, a young man or woman is ready to go to work on a book of poems of his own. Or he may choose to go on to other courses to prepare to become a teacher of poetry so that still other young men and women can go to work.

Energy

Do words have secret energies waiting to be released like the energies within the atom? If they could escape their immemorial bondage to grammar and syntax and sentence structure and conventional human meaning and do for once what they really wanted to do—if they could make love to one another as free agents, would they bombard the reader with undreamed-of power?

I am haunted by the vision, equally unable to believe it true or to believe it untrue.

Poems as Apples

Reviewers are still talking about good poems and bad poems, still praising a book for not having a bad poem in it. If there are no bad poems in it, then it follows that all the poems must be good.

It's like saying there isn't a bad apple in the barrel, a bad apple being, of course, a rotten apple. But everybody who has ever bought apples knows that many many apples are neither bad enough to be called bad nor good enough to be called good. An apple can be undersized or underripe, can be gnarled or scarred, can have a bad spot which if cut out in time leaves the rest of the apple entirely good, and the good half will taste as good in applesauce as the flesh of entirely good apples.

Why is it that farmers and grocers are sometimes more discriminating than book reviewers?

My Life

I used to have a talk which I called "Rome without Camera," but which other people sometimes referred to as "Rome without a Camera."

Perhaps they thought they were improving my title. Or perhaps they thought it didn't make any difference. Or perhaps they didn't think at all.

But to me it did make a difference. It made a difference in balance, rhythm, and economy. I was almost ready to lay down my life to keep my title inviolate.

Caught in a Corner

It was at a cocktail party that a certain woman caught me in a corner.

"What is the difference between a nonpoem and an antipoem?" she demanded.

At first I couldn't be quite sure of what she was saying, such being the noise around me. But by placing her mouth close to mine and repeating the question with assurance, she made herself heard.

"I really don't know," I shouted.

"Oh, come now," she coaxed, offering me a soft dip with crackers, "have a try."

"May I ask if you are asking for information? Or do you know the answer and are only sounding out my ignorance?"

"I consider that an unfair question," she retorted. "Not to say impertinent."

"Forgive me," I pleaded. "But if I must reveal my ignorance, I'd say that a nonpoem was anything not a poem, a poached egg on toast, for example."

I could see that this answer displeased her violently, but having just filled her mouth with soft dip and crackers, she was unable for the moment to do anything but look angry.

"Whereas an antipoem," I continued, "might be a bullet or a puff of poison gas."

"Isn't he bright!" she chirped, having recovered her speech. "But can't you do better than that?"

"I'll try," I said. "It seems to me that the difference between a nonpoem and an antipoem is a perfect question for a woman to catch a man in a corner with."

With a very cool smile she turned her back.

The Trouble with Pegasus

The trouble with Pegasus is not that he is a horse and a very old horse to boot. The trouble with Pegasus is that he is a fraud and a fake.

If the familiar picture of him (such as is used by the Academy of American Poets) has any truth to it, Pegasus never flies, never even gets off the ground. He is represented as a husky beast worthy of plough or chariot, but his wings are those of a cupid.

The Trojan Horse was a fake too, but a fake that was soon found out. Pegasus still enjoys a fairly respectable reputation.

Am I too harsh? There are, of course, ways of defending Pegasus. One can say he was never intended really to fly but only to suggest flight, to symbolize flight, to dream of flying. Pegasus the dreamer, the sentimentalist. But this interpretation leaves him a fake still, albeit a fancy one.

A better defense is to say that once upon a time he actually did fly and kept on flying, but that for many years now his wings have been shrinking till they have become mere vestigial appendices. Pegasus is not so much a fraud as an anachronism.

Perhaps I am too harsh, and of course I am aware that everything I have been saying about Pegasus is being said by somebody or other about poetry itself.

Poetry

Poetry is a dialogue between poet and reader, and poetry is the distillation of solitude. Poetry is madness and poetry is the white light of sanity. Poetry comes from God, and poetry comes from the guts. Poetry is Truth with a capital *T,* and poetry is a pack of lies. Poetry is dead, and poetry is immortal.

*

Neither

I remember so well how he looked when he said it and how they looked when they heard it. They had asked him the old chestnut.

"Do you write for yourself or for an audience?"

"Neither," he answered mildly.

Sputtering surprise. "Well, who—who *do* you write for?"

"I write for God."

Anthologists

Anthologists are by derivation flower gatherers, but flower gathering hardly suggests the seriousness of their pursuit. It would be more accurate to liken them to bees, whose seriousness and industry are proverbial.

Like bees they are innumerable. No one knows how many may be working at any time, for anthologists often work secretly for years before coming into the light.

Perhaps they are more like moles or earthworms than bees, laboring out of sight and sound but destined ultimately to change the very ground we stand on. In the long run anthologists can be profoundly subversive.

For after the critics have decided who the real poets are—the pure, the important, the immortal—the anthologists come along with a rather different answer. They are less interested in poet than in poem; and less interested in the pedigree of a poem than in its readability. If critics are aristocrats, writing for the few about the few, anthologists are usually democrats, writing for the many and hoping for a good sale.

They will, of course, include the immortal poets whenever possible; but they are just as willing to include the mortal. Yeats will doubtless be there, but next door to Yeats will be someone we never heard of before. And even Yeats may be reduced to one little eight-line poem to a squirrel.

For a strictly topical anthology, say, about baseball, the anthologist will have to be very eclectic and wide ranging indeed. Baseball poems must be taken where they can be found, with little help from Shakespeare, Milton, or T. S. Eliot. In a baseball book Marianne Moore will be happily on one page, but just as happy to keep her company will be some newspaper poet, some country versifier.

Thus the critical canon, little by little, gets undermined in spite of the critics, who are, by any count, far fewer than the anthologists.

The Disposable Poem

A distinction should be made between the disposable poem and the poem that time has disposed of. Of all the poems written and published throughout the ages (or written and unpublished) the overwhelming preponderance have been disposed of, in one way or another, by time. Yet from internal evidence—after a little archaeological probing on our part—it is clear that these poems didn't want to be disposed of. They wanted to go on shining in use. They hoped for immortality.

By contrast the disposable poem, so common today, does not hope for immortality, does not look forward to prolonged use, but with a charming modesty and disarming lack of ambition is content to be discarded—or so it seems—after a single reading . . . like the disposable napkin, the disposable handkerchief, the disposable diaper.

Wordman

Sometimes I think I would be just as happy if I were not called a poet. Poets, as we are constantly reminded today, are not just people who write poems, but special people. In other words, "poet" connotes as well as denotes. I would be content with a word that merely denoted.

Especially would I be happier not to have to call myself a poet. Some stubbornly plainer word would serve me better. A woodsman is a man who works in the woods. A postman is a man who works in or out of the post office. A wordman would be a man who works with words. There are many categories of wordman, to be sure, but I do not see that I need be more specific.

So let me be called a wordman and let what I write be called word arrangements. Though this or that critic might deny that I am a poet (a poet, that is, who is more than someone who writes poems), he could scarcely deny that I work with words. As wordman I trust I would not threaten or irritate anyone.

There are a great many poets in the world today, and promise of many, many more to come. By removing myself from the lists, would I not be helping—if only as a gesture—to relieve the crowding?

The Multipurpose Room

When I learned that my reading at the University of Michigan was to be held in the Multipurpose Room, I was a little apprehensive. I pictured the place as a combination of snack bar, lounge, locker room, and laundromat. I wondered how my poetry, how anybody's poetry, could compete with all the other things going on. But at least it would be a striking test of the power of poetry to hold its own in the hustle and bustle of American life. And being a test, it was for me a challenge.

I was, therefore, a little disappointed as well as vastly relieved to find the Multipurpose Room filled with orderly rows of chairs and the chairs filled with a seemingly single-purpose audience.

Poet as Parrot

When at last I had a book of poems and began to be asked to give readings, I took my book with me for more than the obvious reason. It was a prop in the sense of moral support. With that small book in my hand I felt safe. Even when it was closed and I was trying a bit of impromptu interlude, I knew I had only to open it and instantly I would be on firm ground again.

It was also a prop in the sense of stage property. It gave me something to do with my hands. And after I had read a poem, the searching for the next one provided the right interval of silence. Just to turn the pages was a pleasure, suggesting that among so many treasures it was not always easy to pick and choose. A pleasant little book in its quiet green jacket.

My second book of poems changed the situation. To carry around two books looked a little ostentatious. And by that time I knew most of my poems by heart. Why not face my audience without any prop at all?

But the result was not altogether happy. Some people seemed to think my memory more remarkable than the poems memorized.

So I went back to taking a book with me, either book, from which I sometimes read and sometimes pretended to read.

Lemuel Beaver

He is something of a bore, yet I can't really dislike him. A man with such a fresh outlook is bound to be a little refreshing.

He seems to think that anything having to do with poetry will be of interest to me. So, lest I overlook an item or two, he fills me in, he brings me up to date.

Did I know that young poet So-and-So had been arrested for possessing drugs? Or had I heard that Such-and-Such, the literary bigwig, had come out with the frank admission that poetry was dead?

I think he saves up these tidbits for me.

Usually he has the last word as well as the first, but not always. Yesterday instead of news he had a challenge.

"You poets," he began, "say any damn thing that comes into your head. Take the moon, for instance."

"Yes," I murmured, "take the moon."

"You call it a bright penny or a beautiful woman or a ship or a balloon or a goddess or God knows what. Don't you?"

"We do," I admitted, "and the remarkable thing is that everything we say about the moon is true. Isn't it?"

Poetry Workshop

An order for a dozen sonnets has recently come in, and the master is apportioning the work among his journeymen writers and apprentices. Since the sonnets are to form a sequence, he has himself chosen the overall theme and sketched the subsidiary themes of the individual poems.

Some of his most able craftsmen are being entrusted with an entire sonnet apiece. Others are doing preparatory work on rhyme schemes and literary allusion. Most of the apprentices are engaged in research on sonnet sequences of the past for the sake of suggestions and to avoid possible duplication. One sonnet already nearing completion has been posted on the bulletin board for general criticism and final polishing.

Throughout the shop there is a pleasant harmonious hum of activity.

A Little Thinking

Among the contributors to a recent issue of the *Kenyon Review* [vol. 1, 1968] is a man described as "bullfighter, hypnotist, and clairvoyant."

My first reaction upon reading these three words was one of total discouragement. But a little thinking helped to make things better, as it so often does.

After all, was I not myself something of a clairvoyant, though my clear-seeing might have less to do with the future than with the appearance of some small flower in today's sun?

As a hypnotist couldn't I modestly claim to have held the attention of a few readers from time to time?

And as for bullfighting, what was this but another name for a poet's regular job of purifying the language of the tribe?

The Puritan in Me

It must be the puritan in me that responds to the challenge to purify the language of the tribe. Presumably even the lowliest poet can assist in this job, acting like a small auxiliary filter in the water supply system. I should like to think that my poems, whatever else they have failed to be and do, have been performing this useful service.

But I am not at all sure. I am not even clear as to just what impurities I should be trying to purify out. If it is the living language we want, then I should be favoring the loose slangy lingo of the man in the street and filtering out whatever is precise, elegant, and correct. As I say, I am not at all clear.

Even if I knew what I was supposed to be filtering out, how could I be sure that I was actively connected with the main system and that I was purifying anything beyond my own poor poems?

A Passable Sonnet

The phrase catches my eye. Just what would a passable sonnet be? And how could one confidently distinguish a passable sonnet from one not passable?

Would a passable sonnet be a correct sonnet that followed faithfully all the regulation? Or might it be a bold sonnet bent on breaking the rules? Would it be a graceful, elegant sonnet facing the past, or a living, breathing sonnet confronting the present?

The phrase comes from "The academic revolution," whose amiable authors suggest that for a Ph.D. candidate in English it might be more to the point to write a passable sonnet than to learn Anglo-Saxon. They do not go so far as to recommend that a passable sonnet be required of the candidates; they merely suggest that he be required to try to produce one. In other words, both passable and nonpassable sonnets would pass muster if the candidate really tried.

Computers

Several years ago someone tried to put Emily Dickinson through a computer and found that it didn't work. Not very well, anyway.

I should like to think that incompatibility with computers was one proof of the poet, but I'm afraid that the situation may be changing. Just give the computers a few more years.

Towers

In our rejection of the ivory tower we may be overlooking the virtues of towers not ivory.

A tower is not necessarily or primarily for retreat or escape. From a tower one will probably see more of the actual world than from the ground. And in a tower, above the noise and fumes of traffic, one might find the right place for any serious solitary work. Such a tower could be of any convenient material.

The Death of Poetry

"If poetry is really dead," I told him, "then my own poetry is dead and I myself along with it—at least as a poet."

He smiled a little to himself before saying anything. "You still write poems, don't you, Robert?"

"I still write," I replied.

"And your poems are still being published? And people still buy your books and read them? As long as that happens poetry can't be altogether dead, can it?"

"I hope not," I said.

"And what is true of you is true of thousands of other poets. If poetry really is dead, its corpse is strangely full of life and kicking."

"Perhaps poetry is only dying," I suggested. "Dead or dying—it doesn't seem to make much difference to some people. But a dying man can do all sorts of things a dead man can't: draw up a will, make his peace with God, and kiss his wife good-bye. If poetry is only dying, perhaps I can still sing a few small swan songs."

"Of course you can," he assured me. "Of course."

"But if poetry is already dead," I said, "I do wish they'd give it a decent burial."

Suddenly a new thought seemed to strike him. "Have you ever wondered why this announcement of death comes with such assurance? And so untearfully?"

"No," I said. "Why does it?"

"Well, take Blank as an example. Having dried up as a poet himself, he mistakes his own death for the death of poetry."

"Do you really think so?" I asked.

"Or take Double Blank. He still writes, but his poetry belongs to a time long past. Because his sort of poetry is dead, he assumes all poetry is."

"Aren't you being a bit unkind?" I asked.

"Certainly," he said. "The unkindest thing in all the world is truth."

For several minutes we were both silent.

"But we haven't touched the real problem," he mused.

"The trouble with poetry is not that it is dead or dying. The trouble with poetry is that it hasn't died often enough. If poetry doesn't keep on dying, how can it go on being reborn?"

J. P. K.

Suppose Keats had a middle name, John Pennington
Keats. Or more Britishly, J. P. Keats. Or possibly, J.
Pennington Keats, Jr.

Will No One Stand Up for the Adjective?

One should associate with nouns and verbs, we are told, and not with adjectives. With nouns and verbs one can't go wrong, but adjectives lead to excess. The fewer adjectives the better.

Dear me, dear me, when I think of all the beautiful adjectives I know—the fascinating, delectable, mouth-watering, irresistible adjectives. Must I renounce them all? And must I also eliminate all those little everyday, useful-about-the-house adjectives too? If so, how can I make clear that it is hot water I want, not cold water? How can I draw the line between good men and bad men? How can I tell the story of the three bears?

An Experiment

When his poems were rejected by the first publisher he sent them to, he leaped from a high bridge. He was very young and very much the poet.

But he was fished out, brought back to life, and given dry clothing. And since something more was obviously needed, the Rotary Club took him under their wing. They arranged with a local bookstore for him to sit in a show window several hours a day and write poems for sale. It would be good for the poet and good for the bookstore.

The poet did not have the strength to say no. As far as he was concerned he had died and was now living a sort of future life in which he did not know or greatly care how to behave. He submitted.

So they took most of the books out of the window and put the poet in. He sat at a small table with typewriter before him. He sat with his back to the window. People outside could watch his back but could not see his face. They could watch him write but could not see what he was writing. If he seemed something of a goldfish, it was a goldfish who never had to look out of his bowl and meet the gaze of people looking in.

Since he had to make at least a show of writing, he began putting words down almost at random. Surprisingly they turned into little poems without much trouble on his part. Some were miniature love poems, others were seasonal observations, others still something else. He tried a few haiku and discovered that though hard to do very well they were not hard to do rather well. Indeed he gained such facility with haiku that he sometimes found he had written one before he was aware of it. He tried a sonnet.

When these poems, neatly typed, were displayed in the window, the crowd outside the window increased. People began coming in to buy. Prices were not too high, neither were they very low, for after all the buyer was not buying a mere copy, but the poem itself, the whole poem, the only copy, with which he was free to do anything he pleased except to publish it.

Before long the poet—such was his newfound confidence—was offering poems written to order, personalized poems. They would cost somewhat more, of course, than the ready-made.

From every point of view the project was a success. It was more successful than even the Rotary Club had anticipated. In fact, it was almost too successful, for its very success was its ending. So adept had the poet become in dashing off salable poems that he didn't need all the time allotted for it. He found time for himself and, without telling anyone what he was doing, used that time for his own writing. His new poems proved better than those in his first (unpublished) book; and when they were submitted to the publisher who had rejected that book, they were accepted. The poet left the bookstore window. He had graduated.

If this seems too fantastic to believe, consider what that bookstore window had done for the young poet. First, it had given him the gratification of being noticed. Second, it had given him a sense of importance, of being needed, of belonging. Third, it had given him abundant practice in his art. And fourth, it had given him the pleasure of earning money from his art.

But this was not all. Though no one had foreseen it or was quite aware of it when it happened, that window had given the poet everything a poet needs. He had a first-rate typewriter and plenty of paper, he had a lamp that shed on him a privacy of light, he had a comfortable chair. Not only was he undisturbed and undistracted, he had the assurance of remaining so hour after hour. Yet all the while that he was busy at his typewriter, undisturbed and undistracted, he knew that close behind him, though unheard and unseen, was his audience, curious, envious, mocking, hopeful, asking him, begging him, daring him, defying him, to write.

Dates

In the year that Shelley died Matthew Arnold was born. In the year that Matthew Arnold died T. S. Eliot was born. In the year that T. S. Eliot died. . . .

Handwriting

He had called himself a seeker, but when the poem was in print "seeker" had become "sucker."

He was very young at the time and suffered as only the very young can.

Years later it dawned on him that "sucker" was the better word.

Deception

Whenever my poems are called "simple," they are never called simply "simple" but always "deceptively simple." Wherein lies the deception?

Being simple to read, do they seem to have been simple to write? Is this where the deceiving lies?

Or do they only seem simple to read? Are they really not simple at all?

Or are they both truly simple and truly poetry, and is it the possibility of this combination that deceives, or rather undeceives, the reader?

The Great World

Doesn't every poet secretly hope that at least one of his poems will one day rise from the printed page and go forth to action in the great world? If it is too much to hope that it will be sung on the lips of armies like the "Marseillaise" or the "Battle Hymn of the Republic," or that it will save a superannuated battleship from demolition as did Oliver Wendell Holmes's poem "Old Ironsides," then at least that some congressman from the Middle West, reading his local newspaper at breakfast along with the *New York Times,* may come upon it as he sips his coffee and decide then and there to enter it in the *Congressional Record.*

The Robert Poets

Robert would seem a good name for a poet, at least here in America. Among the living, consider the versatile Robert Penn Warren, the classical Robert Fitzgerald, the weighty Robert Kelly, and the towering Robert Bly. Yes, consider Robert Bagg, Robert Creeley, Robert Duncan, Robert Pack, Robert Phillips, Robert Tucker, Robert Wallace, and who knows how many other Robert poets that do not come to mind at the moment. Could it be that the Roberts, by a sort of unconscious conspiracy, are taking over American poetry in the second half of the twentieth century?

Across the water the Roberts that one thinks of first are from the past: Robert Herrick, Robert Burns, Robert Browning, and Robert Bridges. But the present is not unrepresented, for the protean figure of Robert Graves is surely worth half a dozen ordinary Roberts.

Francis

Francis Scott Key: "The Star-Spangled Banner"

Samuel Francis Smith: "My Country 'Tis of Thee"

Robert Churchill Francis:

Hardihood

The following item appeared in the *Daily Telegraph* of July 5, 1968.

The 1st Dorchester Scout Troop are making their own miniature contribution to the Hardy Festival which opens at Dorchester on Sunday. On Wednesday afternoon they are holding a "world record event" in the shape of a non-stop reading of Thomas Hardy's [1000] poems.

Collected Poems

The publication of collected poems must be an ordeal with the best of luck, an ordeal which most poets, of course, never have a chance to undergo. Putting all one's eggs into one basket may be dangerous but not so dangerous as putting all one's poems into one book.

The original books, the little volumes, out of which collected poems are made, leave the poet room to maneuver. If his third volume was panned by reviewers, he can fall back on his first and second for support. And he can lean forward on his fourth and the future. Even selected poems give him some leeway. But with collected poems there is no loophole for escape. He is all there, all sewed up.

If you study the prefaces to collected poems, you will see how various poets meet the problem. Sandburg entertains the reader with a long ramble so readable that one overlooks the self-defense. Frost gives us four nuggety pages. Stevens not a word. It is as if there had been a preface to his collected poems but he had waved a wand and it had vanished.

A Lucky Generation

"The poems of M— P— speak with originality and power for the generation young enough to reject the bland fatuities of the middle aged—"

I pause for breath. I am middle aged myself, or I was not long ago. If middle age gives us bland fatuity, what about old age?

"The poems of M— P— speak with originality and power for the generation young enough to reject the bland fatuities of the middle aged, old enough to have achieved the firmness of full maturity."

What a happy age to be! What a lucky generation! But how long will this mature young poet be able to keep her balance before she too slips into bland fatuity herself?

The *New Yorker* Home Treasury of Verse

The New Yorker Book of Poems came the other day. Nine hundred poems, 835 pages, 3¼ pounds. And I had always thought the *New Yorker* exclusive.

To Wield the Pen

If the poet laureateship were made hereditary, how many headaches could be avoided.

Surely inheritance, which has succeeded century after century in producing rulers of the British Empire could be trusted to write a few verses.

Why shouldn't the present laureate even now be grooming his eldest son or daughter to wield the pen?

Golden Edith

She was, in roughly equal proportions, the actress and the abbess, the queen and the witch.

Scores of her contemporaries rivaled or surpassed her as poet; but no one could touch her as a figure.

In an age when poets were uniformly drab, she was as gaudy as a peacock.

But her triumph was not her costume. Her triumph was to make that costume indigenous and inevitable.

She carried about with her the spaciousness of history. She was high gothic and modern.

If she made an art of arrogance and insult, it was only as an aristocrat can.

Her touch was as golden as Midas's. In her *Collected Poems* you can count the word *gold* 280 times and the world *golden* 94. In anyone else this might have seemed too easy.

Without her poems we would be appreciably poorer, but without herself we would be defrauded.

The Reversible Dictum

"It begins in delight and ends in wisdom," says Frost of a poem. I was going to call this a good illustration of the reversible dictum. Turn it around and it is equally true. It begins in wisdom and ends in delight.

That's what I was going to say. But then I thought how few poems today begin in either wisdom or delight, end in either, or have either in the middle.

A Wide Wide World

"Alps beyond Alps arise," sang Pope, and the same thing could be said of poets. They keep rising into view— beyond the Alleghenies, beyond the Mississippi, beyond the Rockies. Only today I learn of a certain peak that has been looming in the poetry world these many years. Where have I been? And who am I?

Horticulture

"He was a poet, but no more concerned with poetry than a plant is concerned with horticulture," says Wallace Fowlie of Cocteau.

Alas! how much concerned with horticulture many a modern plant seems to be.

On the Moon

Fort Juniper
Amherst, Mass.
December 12, 1969

Dear Nicholas,

I should like to accept your gracious invitation to contribute to *Polymus,* but I am not clever enough to sit down and dash off a poem on any subject. Poems must first come to me and ask me to help them to get born. And birth takes a little time.

However, I do have a poem on the moon already born and even published. I think you could get permission to reprint it in *Polymus* if this were not against your editorial policy and if you happened to take to the poem. It is found in my latest collection, *Come Out Into the Sun: Poems New and Selected,* published by the University of Massachusetts Press in 1965. It has an unusually long title: "Edith Sitwell Assumes the Role of Luna, or If You Know What I Mean Said the Moon."

Several years ago I got to wondering how the moon would feel and think about man's tinkerings, if she really were a goddess. Having written the poem, I discovered that the moon had talked like Edith Sitwell, not in her poems but in her various public pronouncements. So I had to include Dame Edith in the title. Result: what Edith would say if she thought she were the moon, or what the moon might say if she fancied herself Edith.

If you are interested, write to Paul M. Wright, Editor, The University of Massachusetts Press, Munson Hall, Amherst, Mass., 01002, explaining the whole situation and telling him I hope he might see his way clear to granting you permission to reprint without reprint fee.

Otherwise, I hope you will invite me to have a part in some later, and less restrictive, number. I think I would find it difficult, dear Nicholas, not to give you anything you asked for.

Peace,

Gift Copies

"It gets worse and worse," he said.

"What gets worse and worse, Theophilus?"

"The giving of gift copies."

I looked at him in amazement, yet he seemed serious.

"I can't believe it," I exclaimed. "Giving copies of your books to friends ought to be one of the great joys of life. In fact, a threefold joy. First, there is the joy of writing poems. Second, the joy of having them published. Third, the joy of giving."

He still looked unhappy.

"I suppose what you mean is that there are now so many people who want gift copies and would feel slighted not to have them that you can't meet the demand."

"It's not that," he said. "The trouble is not with slighting people but with annoying them. There are people who would feel hurt not to be remembered yet not altogether happy when they are."

"What on earth are you talking about?" I cried.

Theophilus did not answer immediately. "You see," he began a little reluctantly, "to receive a gift copy from the author does put a man in a spot. To thank the author-donor one should have read the book or at least part of it. Not only read it, but enjoyed it. But suppose one hasn't enjoyed it? And doesn't want to make the effort to try to?"

It was my turn to be silent.

"I can't really blame anyone," Theophilus added. "After all, I have received gift copies myself."

Theophilus Again

"Do you remember," I asked my poet friend Theophilus, "your telling me some time ago about your experience in being introduced to audiences and of your technique for defending yourself against the exuberance of your introducer?"

"I do," said Theophilus.

"What I want to ask is why a poet needs any introduction at all. Why doesn't he simply get up and begin? Why does he need someone to explain him, to defend him, and to praise him? Why does the audience need a pep talk before the poetry? Even the introducer often has the sense to say that the poet of the evening needs no introduction. Why doesn't he abide by his own good sense?"

"A good question," said Theophilus. "A very good question indeed."

John Peale Bishop, John Crowe Ransom, and Robert Penn Warren

Of these three only Robert Penn Warren has an accurately functional middle name. I imagine that John Peale Bishop never once in his life did any pealing. And as for John Crowe Ransom, you never would have caught that fine gentleman crowing.

Invoice to Go with a
Gift Copy of My Poems

A box of homemade cookies is a safer gift than a book of homemade poems. But if you will not feel the least obligation to read this book, or if you read it, to like it, the danger of burdening you may not be too great.

Let it sit in the chimney corner like Cinderella or in some obscure nook of your library, and when your eye happens to fall on it from time to time let it bring a smile to your lips as you remember its author.

E. D.

In spite of Emily Dickinson's world renown, in spite of all the books about her and her poetry, she is still mysterious. For instance, incredible as it may seem, it is not generally known even today that one of her books won both the Pulitzer Prize and the National Book Award, and escaped the Bollingen Prize only by a hair. Indeed, had she lived a year or two longer there is every reason to believe she would have become a Nobel Laureate, even though in her day women were less likely than today to be crowned anything but queen.

That Emily was unpublished and unknown during her lifetime is a legend planted and watered by the poet herself. Actually she had everything: grants, fellowships, awards, prizes, and not inconsiderable royalties. Was she not for a time Consultant in Poetry at the Library of Congress and often an honored guest at the White House? Without funding from such corporations as Amoco and Exxon it is doubtful she would have gone on writing poetry.

To a *Time* reporter she once whispered: "Whitman says it takes great audiences to produce great poetry. *I* say it takes great cash."

Of course it was immensely shrewd of the little Belle of Amherst to conceal all this. How successful she was in her strategy is evident today when she is still spoken of and written about as a shy little violet.

Magic

Poets used to be thought of as magicians, pulling out of their hat of words something surprising and delightful.

Today many poets eschew magic. Instead of a mysterious rabbit, they give us the hat itself, the empty hat, the old hat with the sweaty hatband. After all (they seem to be reminding us) no hat we really wear has a rabbit in it.

Emily

In Amherst when someone leans out of a car window and asks the way to Emily's grave, one does not ask, "Emily who?"

Again the Rose

"The rose by any other name would smell as sweet," said Juliet.

"True," affirms the semanticist. "Very true."

"Untrue," says the poet, Juliet and Shakespeare notwithstanding. "A rose by any other name would indeed smell sweet, but not quite so sweet. It would not have that specifically rosy sweetness that it has been acquiring over the centuries."

So the semanticist does everything he can to separate words from what words stand for, while the poet does everything he can to make words and meanings identical.

Essentially a difference between science and magic.

For Queens

Reading Richard Wilbur's celebrated poem, "Walking to Sleep," I find myself pausing over the first line.

As queens sit down, knowing that a chair will be there.

Surely to sit down without looking to see what is there to sit on is a queenly prerogative. And over the ages countless queens may have done just that, with seldom if ever a mishap. Just the same, the world being what it now is, I should like to say to all existing queens that it would be wiser to look first.

Byron, Kelly, and Sheets

She had uttered the three names together so many times over the years that they had become fixed, inseparable, a trade name like a firm of lawyers or clothiers.

So when she stood before the literary section of the women's club one afternoon and announced the subject of her talk, the three names came so naturally to her tongue that she did not need to think of what she was saying.

She was a meek little body of a high-school English teacher, and when the ladies tittered (as some of them must have) she must have blushed deeply.

Landor

"I strove with none," said Walter Savage Landor in his immortal quatrain, "for none was worth my strife."

Actually he seems to have striven with just about everybody. There is the story of his picking up a man-servant and throwing him out the window in Florence. And exclaiming a moment later: "My God, the violets!"

The Discoverer

I once heard a man tell Robert Frost to his face that he had a sense of humor.

It was at Bread Loaf years ago. Someone in the audience who was hearing Frost for the first time came up to congratulate him after the reading. With the air of a discoverer he exclaimed:

"Mr. Frost, you have a wonderful sense of humor."

Frost recoiled, blinked, and gave his head a little shake as if unprepared for the shock.

So the man repeated his discovery. "Man, I'm telling you. A wonderful sense of humor."

Yes, Why?

"Why don't you write confessional poetry yourself?" he was saying. "You've been bottled up goodness knows how many years. Why don't you take off the lid and let yourself go?"

"Yes," I murmured. "Why don't I?"

"You are a deep well of pure cold water. You are both the well and the drawer of water, bringing up bucketful after bucketful."

"Or cupful by cupful," I interposed.

"Why don't you now become a fountain and just flow? Flow and overflow?"

"Yes," I went on. "Why don't I splash in the sunlight and spill over the stone pavement, so that pigeons may come and drink and coo and cool their feathers, and little kids with toy boats, and old men and women, and lovers—?"

Festivals

When I think of the poetry festivals I have attended and taken part in, my mind goes back to the Book of Hosea, the twelfth chapter, the first verse:

> Ephraim feedeth on wind.

Elegy

It was only the other day
We had Stephen Vincent Benet
And Edna St. Vincent Millay.

Luxury Cruise

It is an excellent book, erudite, comprehensive, original, witty. Indeed I can't imagine a more outstanding volume in its field. My only fault with it is its name. It is called *An Introduction to Poetry.*

Far from being a mere introduction, it is nothing less than a personally conducted, year-long, tour of poetry on a luxury liner with four swimming pools (two indoors, two out), five restaurants, seven night clubs, and fifty snack bars, guaranteeing at least twenty things to do at any moment and touching at the world's thirty most glamorous ports.

A League

There used to be a league and it may still be in existence, though I haven't heard it mentioned for many a year. All I remember is that it was a league and that it was devoted to poetry.

Was it the League to Support Poetry? Or, the League to Promote Poetry? Or was it the League to Defend Poetry? Or possibly the League to Protect Poetry?

Friends of the Francis

If a poet is really a cultural institution as is often intimated, should he not have a supporting organization, some sort of auxiliary that would raise money in small amounts from school children and others so that the poet might enjoy now a new tape recorder, and now a fresh coat of paint on his house?

Local Poet

The phrase is ambiguous. It may mean merely that the poet happens to live in the same locality that you do. Or it may mean that the poet is confined to that locality, unknown beyond it.

In the current issue of my local newspaper mention is made of "two local poets." Here the implication seems to be that the two are only a sample and that a dozen more might easily be named if one wanted to go to the bother. The locality is Amherst, Massachusetts.

But the phrase could mean something quite different. It could mean that the local poet not only lives here but that his poetry lives here too. It could mean that his poems have roots as well as blossoms. In this sense Dante is very much a local poet. So is Wordsworth and Emily Dickinson and perhaps even T. S. Eliot.

Poetry is the excitement produced by the unexpected becoming the inevitable. But in poetry of the past, though there was much of the inevitable, there was sometimes little of the unexpected; while in poetry today, though there is plenty of the unexpected, sometimes there is no inevitability at all.

Dionysus: They are all my poets now, Apollo.

Apollo: Not quite all, Dionysus.

Dionysus: You had them for a long time, Apollo.

Apollo: And there's a long time still to come, Dionysus.

UNDER DISCUSSION
Donald Hall, General Editor

Volumes in the Under Discussion series collect reviews and essays about individual poets. The series is concerned with contemporary American and English poets about whom the consensus has not yet been formed and the final vote has not been taken. Titles in the series include:

Elizabeth Bishop and Her Art
edited by Lloyd Schwartz and Sybil P. Estess
Richard Wilbur's Creation *edited and with an*
Introduction by Wendy Salinger
Reading Adrienne Rich
edited by Jane Roberta Cooper
On the Poetry of Allen Ginsberg
edited by Lewis Hyde
Robert Bly: When Sleepers Awake
edited by Joyce Peseroff

Forthcoming volumes will examine the work of Robert Creeley, H.D., Galway Kinnell, and Louis Simpson, among others.

Please write for further information on available editions and current prices.

Ann Arbor   **The University of Michigan Press**